Our Diverse Middle School Students

Learn how to be more responsive to the diversity among your middle schoolers. This important book, co-published with the Association for Middle Level Education (AMLE), helps you understand racial, ethnic, linguistic, socioeconomic, gender, intellectual, and social aspects of diversity, and consider how they relate to the unique needs and development of young adolescents. Each chapter begins with a brief case study, followed by background information, questions to consider, practical strategies, and appendices with additional resources. With the helpful advice in this book, you'll be better prepared to create a more equitable learning environment for all.

Elizabeth D. Dore, Ed.D. is recently retired from Radford University (VA) as a full professor in the School of Education and Leadership. She was the coordinator of middle-level teacher education for 14 years, teaching classes in educational psychology, adolescent development, classroom management, assessment, and supervising middle school pre-service students in both early field experience and student teaching.

Deborah H. McMurtrie, Ph.D. is an associate professor in the School of Education at the University of South Carolina Aiken. She is the university's middle-level education program coordinator and teaches courses in educational psychology, adolescent development, classroom management, assessment, and teaching diverse populations in the middle and high school. She is a certified teacher with more than 25 years of teaching experience.

D1591321

Also Available from AMLE and Routledge
(www.routledge.com/k-12)

Content Area Literacy Strategies That Work:
Do This, Not That!
Lori G. Wilfong

The Flexible SEL Classroom:
Practical Ways to Build Social-Emotional Learning in Grades 4-8
Amber Chandler

Our Diverse Middle School Students

A Guide to Equitable and Responsive Teaching

Elizabeth D. Dore, Ed.D., and
Deborah H. McMurtrie, Ph.D.

Routledge
Taylor & Francis Group

NEW YORK AND LONDON

First published 2021
by Routledge
52 Vanderbilt Avenue, New York, NY 10017

and by Routledge
2 Park Square, Milton Park, Abingdon, Oxon, OX14 4RN

Routledge is an imprint of the Taylor & Francis Group, an informa business

Library of Congress Cataloging-in-Publication Data
Names: Dore, Elizabeth D., 1943- author. | McMurtrie, Deborah H., author.
Title: Our diverse middle school students : a guide to equitable and responsive teaching / Dr. Elizabeth D. Dore, Dr. Deborah H. McMurtrie.
Description: New York, NY : Routledge, 2021. | Includes bibliographical references.
Identifiers: LCCN 2020041164 | ISBN 9780367510893 (hardback) | ISBN 9780367507961 (paperback) | ISBN 9781003052371 (ebook)
Subjects: LCSH: Culturally relevant pedagogy. | Middle school students. | Multicultural education.
Classification: LCC LC1099.515.C85 D67 2021 | DDC 370.117--dc23
LC record available at https://lccn.loc.gov/2020041164

ISBN: 978-0-367-51089-3 (hbk)
ISBN: 978-0-367-50796-1 (pbk)
ISBN: 978-1-003-05237-1 (ebk)

Typeset in Palatino
by KnowledgeWorks Global Ltd.

Portions of this book were previously published by the National Middle School Association as *Diversity and Young Adolescents: More Than Color*, © 2004.

This book is dedicated to my late husband, who was always a rock when doubt and questions raised their heads in my writing and thinking.

—Betty Dore

To my four amazing daughters—Lauren, Lindsey, Caitlin, and Kelly—who challenged and enriched my understandings of adolescence in ways I never imagined.

—Deborah McMurtrie

Contents

List of Tables................................... *ix*

Introduction................................... *1*

1 Who Are Middle School Students?................. 3

2 Racial and Ethnic Diversity..................... 8

3 Linguistic Diversity........................... 15

4 Socioeconomic Diversity....................... 24

5 Family Structures............................. 32

6 Physical Diversity............................ 39

7 Gender and Sexual Diversity.................... 47

8 Intellectual Diversity.......................... 59

9 Emotional Diversity........................... 69

10 Social Diversity.............................. 79

11 Geographical Diversity........................ 86

12 Religious Diversity........................... 89

13 Developing a Diverse Curriculum.............. 96

14 Differentiating Instruction................... 104

Conclusion 111

Appendix A: Recommended Adolescent
Literature (Current) 118

Appendix B: Recommended Adolescent
Literature (Classics) 124

Appendix C: Association for Middle Level
Education Standards 136

Appendix D: AMLE Essential Attributes
and Characteristics 138

List of Tables

3.1 Sample Funds of Knowledge Plan   17
3.2 Selected Patterns and Features of
    African American English   20
7.1 Glossary of Gender Terms   50
7.2 Examples of Discriminatory School Policies
    and Practices Based on Gender   53
8.1 Suggested Accommodations for
    Diverse Learners   64
14.1 Suggested Pedagogical Strategies
    for Differentiation   106
14.2 Suggested Assessment Strategies
    for Differentiation   108

Introduction

There are few groups more diverse than young adolescents. Young adolescents develop and change tremendously between the ages of 10 and 15, most visibly in their physical development, but just as importantly in their social, emotional, and cognitive development. This diversity is the middle school experience, but it extends far beyond these characteristics.

Young adolescents are diverse in many ways. Some are obvious, such as race, gender, and socioeconomic status. Some less obvious but equally powerful dimensions of diversity include linguistic differences, family structures, religion, and a wide range of exceptionalities. Included in physical diversity are sexual maturity, rates of growth, and physical disabilities. Social development refers to personality differences, emotional maturity, and impulse control. Cognitive development includes learning modalities and intellectual exceptionalities.

In this book, we explore the nature of diversity and implications for schools and teachers in their classrooms. Each chapter begins with a brief "case study," followed by background information and useful strategies for classroom teachers as they respond to the unique needs of all students. These strategies provide recommended approaches, possible assignments, and resources for each of the major concepts presented.

All young adolescents are diverse—even those who do not appear to be. Classroom teachers today are faced with increasingly diverse students. No longer can they expect to face a group of children who are homogeneous in any way. Rather, they must be prepared to understand students who reflect a wide variety of cultures, traditions, backgrounds, and abilities. Every classroom will challenge teachers with these very interesting and diverse groups of young people. This book will be a stepping-stone to that understanding. It is intended as a supplement to other texts in middle school teacher preparation courses, but it may also be used by veteran classroom teachers looking for effective strategies to reach new and diverse classroom populations. It is a compilation of ideas—old and new. Pre-service teachers, first-year teachers, and veteran teachers will gain insights into the unique characteristics, needs, and interests of young adolescents, and use that knowledge to inform their decisions about developmentally and culturally responsive curriculum and instruction.

This book is also for parents, guardians, and anyone interested in young adolescents. It is for anyone who wants to understand and find ways to help 10- to 15-year-olds become successful young adults.

1

Who Are Middle School Students?

Case Study

Ms. Kelly had always dreamed of being a second-grade teacher. Unfortunately, when she graduated from college, there were no elementary school jobs to be had. The day before school started, she finally got a job offer. It was for a seventh-grade social studies position at Westside Middle School, a high-need, low-income school. She was terrified, but she desperately needed the job so she accepted the offer.

On the first day of school, when the homeroom bell rang, Ms. Kelly looked out at the sea of faces in her classroom. She noticed some of the girls were tall and physically mature, while many of the boys were short and looked very young. Some of the students were dressed in new, trendy clothing, while others wore shabby hand-me-downs. One student near the front of the class wore a hearing aid, while another student with special needs required his own shadow. Some students looked her straight in the eye, but others looked down. A small group of girls spoke quietly in Spanish in the back of the room. More than half of her students were African American. A handful were Asian. One girl wore a hijab; the rest of her students were Latino.

Ms. Kelly, who was white, realized none of the students in the room looked like her. She wondered about the students' backgrounds. What were their families like? What challenges did they face at home and at school? She wondered about their abilities, interests, and needs. She asked herself, "How will I be able to engage, challenge, and support such a diverse group of students?"

Chapter Content

Young adolescents in the 10–15-year-old age group face a period when their lives are surrounded by confusion, disorder, turmoil, chaos, and change. Middle-level students are acutely aware of the smallest differences between their peers and themselves. They undergo rapid changes—physical, social, emotional, and cognitive. One day a young person may be absolutely sure of everything and the next day not sure of anything. Young adolescents find themselves in situations where they are treated neither as children nor as adults. They find themselves wanting to identify as individuals yet routinely conform to dress, attitude, and activities of their peer groups.

Increasingly, young adolescents have to deal with less support from traditional sources. Many times, a single parent has more than one job just to make ends meet; "latchkey kids," with no adult at home after school, are more and more common. Because of the transient nature of families today, there are fewer opportunities for extended family members to provide support for young adolescents. Combine this lack of support with the rapid changes and constant peer pressure young adolescents experience, and it is easy to see the bewildering choices this new stage of life has thrust upon them.

In this book we will discuss a variety of different issues and how they affect young adolescents during a time of great growth. When reflecting on these characteristics, we need to understand the importance of diversity when discussing young adolescents. Just as tadpoles change to frogs, so do our middle schoolers change from young children to young adolescents, and then, to beautiful people. But, they are diverse, each with his or her own kind of beauty.

Young adolescents, who are in schools or classes comprising only one cultural group, need to learn about other cultures and ethnicities in order to be prepared for the world outside their own. As difficult as it is to imagine, there are young people who have never seen anyone who looks different or who thinks differently, until they go away to college or enter the military. Isn't this all the more reason to raise awareness of many types of diversity? When students with physical or intellectual disabilities are mainstreamed in regular classes, both those with and without disabilities learn from each other. Students learn to be more caring, understanding, and aware of individuals and how they can be different; they also learn about their own strengths and weaknesses and how to work and learn together. But, cultures and physical and intellectual abilities and disabilities are not the only qualities which make people diverse. Family makeup—single parents, same-sex parents, adoptive parents, grandparents, parents who work outside the home, family expectations for the young adolescent, and opportunities available to the student—all are diverse situations. Sexual orientation, learning modalities and abilities, and even geographical location and accent may also be included.

One way to help young adolescents learn to accept differences of all kinds—physical, social, emotional, and cognitive—is to make them aware of books and films that can help them understand their own and other cultures. At the same time, they must be careful not to reinforce misconceptions and stereotypes.

No longer are the majority of classrooms filled with students who all live in the same neighborhood, go to the same church, and eat the same food. Students whose second language is English, who wear different clothes, and have different traditions are moving into previously all white neighborhoods at a rapid pace. Teaching approaches and school curricula must be adapted to address this change.

Characteristics of Young Adolescents

- ◆ They are bright and curious.
- ◆ They are sensitive and aware of how they are perceived.
- ◆ They struggle with issues around ethnicity, race, and gender.

- ◆ They respond to support and exhortations to improve.
- ◆ Many assume tremendous responsibilities in their families and church communities, causing them to be more adult-like than many adults expect.
- ◆ They have high aspirations and want well-paying jobs; they do not know the instrumental steps to reach their goals.
- ◆ They are loyal, care about what significant others think of them, and do not want to disappoint these people.
- ◆ They respond to discipline, structure, and consistency.
- ◆ They respond to caring, firm, friendly adults who they trust and respect and by whom they feel cared for and respected.
- ◆ They work when what they are doing has meaning in their daily lives and will help them achieve a goal or a dream.
- ◆ They learn and achieve when taught as if this is expected.
- ◆ Their parents and families are concerned, and use suggestions and respond to coaching from teachers.
- ◆ Their parents and extended families are proud when they do well and support their efforts and achievements.

Questions to Consider

1. Describe six or more dimensions of diversity in today's middle school classrooms. Include individual differences and group differences.
2. Visit a middle school classroom. How would you describe the students in terms of racial, ethnic, and socioeconomic (SES) dimensions or differences?
3. How do the teachers at this school demonstrate they value and respect diversity?
4. If the students are grouped by "ability," what does a gifted and talented classroom look like? What does a special education classroom look like? How are the different races represented in advanced vs. remedial classes?

5. Who are the exceptional and culturally different students in your school? What are the characteristics or factors which make them exceptional and culturally different?

Strategies for Teachers

◆ Listen to your middle school students—REALLY listen.
◆ Learn who they are and what they are about.
◆ What are their hobbies, special abilities, and dreams?
◆ What is their home life like?
◆ What strengths and talents do they bring to the classroom?
◆ Provide opportunities for physical, social, and emotional development.

2

Racial and Ethnic Diversity

Case Study

Diane Parker was a 55-year-old white female who had grown up during the Civil Rights era. As a child, Diane lived in an all-white neighborhood, attended segregated schools, and had limited contact with people of color. Although she didn't like to talk about it, she grew up in a home which explicitly used racist language. This experience, coupled with negative and violent stereotypes of people of color she had seen in the media, reinforced the stereotype—African Americans were poor, uneducated, and deficient.

After staying home to raise three children, Diane had returned to college to finish her degree. She had recently accepted a teaching position at a local middle school, and it was her first day. The culture of this school was foreign to her. In her opinion, the students were loud and disrespectful. They had difficulty sitting still. By the end of third period, she was contemplating quitting. Then, her fourth period class—a gifted and talented (GT) group—arrived. What a difference! These students listened well, spoke 'proper' English, and stayed in their seats. Suddenly, Mrs. Parker realized all of the students in this GT class were white. Later, she asked one of the other teachers about it.

"It seems my classes are all either disproportionately black and brown or white," she said. "Are your classes like that too?"

"Yes," replied the other teacher. "The kids in your lower sections are going to be your discipline problems. Don't hesitate to write them up. After three detentions, those kids will get in-school suspension. Once they are out of your classroom, your job will be much easier."

"Doesn't it seem a bit unfair?" asked Mrs. Parker. "I mean, if they're not in the classroom, they can't learn."

"Do you really want to deal with them?" asked the other teacher.

"I'm not sure," said Mrs. Parker. "I want to help them, but I just don't know how."

Chapter Content

Although many people think racism is a thing of the past, it continues to rear its ugly head, sometimes in insidious ways.

Racism is a system of oppression which is pervasive, restrictive, and hierarchal (Bell, 2010). Racism functions "not only through overt, conscious prejudice and discrimination but also through the unconscious attitudes and behaviors of a society that presumes an unacknowledged but pervasive white cultural norm" (Bell, 2010, p. 24). Thus, racism creates and maintains a dominant power structure.

Perhaps the most urgent challenge facing the nation is "providing high-quality schooling for all students, especially those presently underserved by the educational system, including students of color, low-income students, English language-learners and students in rural and urban settings" (Hollins & Guzman, 2005, p. 477). Indeed, every aspect of our education system, including "teacher demographics, instructional strategies, curriculum, textbooks, disciplinary practices, testing and tracking policies, retention practices, [and] graduation rates" (Chubbuck, 2010, p. 207), contributes to the marginalization and academic failure of many students of color in our society. Disparities in education and the achievement gap are reflected in, among other things, high school graduation rates. According to the most recent Schott Foundation report (2015), the United States' national high school graduation rate for black male students in 2012–2013 was 59%. Many of the states with the lowest graduation rates (<55%) were located in the southeast.

Other troubling national statistics include the percentage of black male high school students, who were suspended from school in 2012–2013 (15%), as compared to a white male suspension rate of 5%. In addition, 14.6% of black males were expelled from school, as compared to only 1.6% of their white counterparts (NCES, 2012). The Schott Foundation "firmly believes that these data are not indicative of a character flaw in black boys and men, but rather they are evidence of an unconscionable level of willful neglect and disparate resource allocations by federal, state and local entities and a level of indifference by too many community leaders" (Schott Foundation for Public Education, 2015, p. 28). We, too, are convinced this is evidence of a systemic problem—we are failing our students of color.

Much of the problem lies in the "demographic divide" (Castro, 2010; Milner, 2008) between teachers and students. In the United States, approximately 82% of teachers are white and middle-class, yet their students are strikingly diverse and becoming more so (NCES, 2012; Zumwalt & Craig, 2005). The mismatch between teachers' and students' racial backgrounds is important because teachers who have limited experience with students of color may misinterpret their students' unfamiliar behaviors and make stereotyped assumptions from a deficit perspective. For example, a teacher may interpret a student's more direct conversational style as being disrespectful or non-compliant, and unilaterally punish the student.

It is well documented that the U.S. schools systematically marginalize and fail many children of color (Kozol, 2005; Kumashiro, 2004/2009; Valenzuela, 1999). Schools continue to reproduce social inequities through racialized structures, practices, and discourses that privilege some students and disadvantage others (Yosso, 2002). Yet these processes are hard to see.

Disparities in funding, access, and achievement in education are intimately tied to race. Everyday practices in schools perpetuate inequities, but the actual processes can be hard to see. If we want to understand why schools continue to reproduce social inequities, we must develop a more complex understanding of the role white teachers play, consciously and unconsciously, in perpetuating institutionalized racism. One way to do this is to routinely analyze the school's referral and suspension data to make sure no one group of students is unfairly singled out.

Gloria Ladson-Billings (2011) contends, "We should question the repeated practice of preparing young, white, suburban, middle-class, monolingual English speakers to teach an increasingly diverse student population" (p. 389). She argues we must address the demographics of teaching by recruiting and retaining more teacher candidates of color. But, we must also address the preparation of white pre-service teachers for increasingly diverse classrooms. Gay (2010) asserts, "Teachers cannot reasonably be expected to meet these challenges if they have not been adequately prepared for them…. [Teacher education programs] must include skills for culturally responsive teaching in their professional development programs" (p. 251).

Teachers operating from a deficit perspective devalue and delegitimize students' cultural knowledge, identity, and heritage (García & Guerra, 2004). Conversely, culturally responsive teachers believe students come to school with knowledge, which is valued and respected, and build on the strengths their students bring to the classroom (Gay, 2010; Ladson-Billings, 2009).

Questions to Consider

1. Do you believe we live in a post-racial society? Why or why not?
2. How were you raised to think about issues related to racial and ethnic diversity? What would you teach your children about these issues?
3. Can you identify key experiences or pivotal moments in your life which shaped your understandings about race and racism?

4. Why is it important for teachers to reflect on their own biases and stereotypes about racial and cultural diversity?

Strategies for Teachers

Analyze children's books for sexism, racism, and stereotyping. The following ideas are suggested by the Council on Interracial Books for Children:

♦ Check for illustrations which are stereotypical or examples of tokenism. Is there a male figure depicted going to work carrying a briefcase, while a female figure stays at home with the children?

♦ Check the story line for standards of success: Does it depict "white" behavior, or resolutions being made only by them?

♦ What is the role of minorities in the business world or in athletics?

♦ Are African Americans depicted only as athletes and musicians?

♦ Examine the characters' lifestyles for inaccuracies, as well as inappropriate or oversimplified depictions of any one culture. For example, are Asians all depicted as small in stature, with dark complexions, and proficient in math?

♦ Consider which character has the power, exhibits leadership, and solves problems in relationships between characters in the story. Is the leader always depicted as a white male, and the person with the problem either female or a minority?

♦ Whose interests are being served by the heroes? Are minority children only portrayed in universal settings or are they actually in their own cultural communities?

♦ What are the effects on self-image of the middle-level students? Do students see persons from their cultures portrayed as heroes or heroines?

♦ Check the author's or illustrator's qualifications. Does this person have expertise in the subject for which he or she is reporting?

- ◆ Do textbook authors depict their own culture as superior?
- ◆ Check for offensive overtones in descriptions and conversations. Are clichés such as "Jew them down on the price," "Indian giver," or "Chinese fire drill" used in conversations or descriptions?
- ◆ Check the copyright date. More recently published books are often less racially offensive.
- ◆ Peruse the local newspaper to find stereotypes in writing and in advertising.

References

Bell, L. A. (2010). Theoretical foundations. In M. Adams, W. J. Blumenfeld, C. Castañeda, H. W. Hackman, M. L. Peters, & X. Zúñiga (Eds.), *Readings for diversity and social justice* (2nd ed., pp. 21–35). New York, NY: Routledge.

Castro, A. J. (2010). Themes in the research on preservice teachers' views of cultural diversity: Implications for researching millennial preservice teachers. *Educational Researcher, 39*(3), 198–210.

Chubbuck, S. M. (2010). Individual and structural orientations in socially just teaching: Conceptualization, implementation, and collaborative effort. *Journal of Teacher Education, 61*(3), 197–210.

García, S., & Guerra, P. (2004). Deconstructing deficit thinking: Working with educators to create more equitable learning environments. *Education and Urban Society, 36*, 150–168.

Gay, G. (2010). *Culturally responsive teaching* (2nd ed.). New York, NY: Teachers College Press.

Hollins, E. R., & Guzman, M. T. (2005). Research on preparing teachers for diverse populations. In M. Cochran-Smith, & K. M. Zeichner (Eds.), *Studying teacher education: The report of the AERA panel on research and teacher education* (pp. 477–548). Mahwah, NJ: Lawrence Erlbaum Associates.

Kozol, J. (2005). *The shame of the nation: The restoration of apartheid schooling in America.* New York, NY: Broadway Paperbacks.

Kumashiro, K. (2004/2009). *Against common sense: Teaching and learning toward social justice.* New York, NY: Routledge.

Ladson-Billings, G. (2009). *The dreamkeepers: Successful teachers of African-American children.* San Francisco, CA: Jossey-Bass.

Ladson-Billings, G. (2011). Asking the right questions: A research agenda for studying diversity in teacher education. In A. F. Ball & C. A. Tyson (Eds.), *Studying diversity in teacher education* (pp. 385–398). Lanham, MD: Rowman & Littlefield Publishers.

Milner, H. R. (2008). Critical race theory and interest convergence as analytic tools in teacher education policies and practices. *Journal of Teacher Education, 59*(4), 332–346.

National Center for Education Statistics (NCES) (2012). Youth indicators. Retrieved from http://nces.ed.gov/pubs2012/2012026/tables/table_14.asp.

Schott Foundation for Public Education (2015). The urgency of now: The Schott 50 state report on public education and black males. Retrieved from http://blackboysreport.org/#.

Valenzuela, A. (1999). *Subtractive schooling: U.S.-Mexican youth and the politics of caring.* Albany, NY: State University of New York Press.

Yosso, T. J. (2002). Toward a critical race curriculum. *Equity & Excellence in Education, 35*(2), 93–107.

Zumwalt, K., & Craig, E. (2005). Teachers' characteristics: Research on the demographic profile. In M. Cochran-Smith, & K. M. Zeichner (Eds.), *Studying teacher education: The report of the AERA panel on research and teacher education* (pp. 111–156)). Mahwah, NJ: Lawrence Erlbaum Associates.

3

Linguistic Diversity

Case Study

Mr. Vince, a white male teacher, was tough on his eighth grade English Language Arts students. He was ruthless with a red pen and was known for marking up papers which didn't adhere to formal, standard American English conventions. One of the errors which drove him crazy was when students left out the '-s' at the end of plural words. One day he complained to another teacher. "I'm constantly correcting these careless mistakes, and the kids just don't get it," he said.

Mrs. Scott, who was standing nearby, jumped in. "Is it just one student?" she asked. Mr. Vince replied, "Actually, it's most of my African American students."

Mrs. Scott said, "And they're all making the very same 'mistake,' over and over again?" Mr. Vince nodded. Mrs. Scott responded, "It doesn't sound like careless errors to me. It sounds like a pattern."

"Well, they write the way they talk," Mr. Vince said. "A dialect might be okay at home, but it's not okay at school." Mrs. Scott said, "Are you saying the way your African American students speak at home is wrong? Or is it just different?"

Chapter Content

When a young adolescent from India, Asia, or Mexico enrolls in an American school, it provides a perfect opportunity to broaden diversity in the classroom. Sometimes, these students come from outstanding schools, but sometimes, they are children of immigrants who, even though they were well-respected and gainfully employed in their native country, find themselves without jobs, unable to understand English, and now living in less than desirable conditions. Teachers need to place these young students in situations where they will succeed, where they will be able to learn English and do well in their school work, and where they will socialize with their peers, regardless of the fact they feel they are different. When a child from India enrolled in one class, the teacher used it as the perfect opportunity to begin a social studies unit on India—its culture, traditions, government, religion, and more. The young girl was able to contribute ideas and information no textbook could ever have supplied. This student was so excited that she felt welcomed and so proud her new peers turned to her for information and asked her questions. It was a successful situation for all involved.

Instead of focusing on the deficiencies of the English language learner (ELL), consider the "funds of knowledge" linguistically diverse students bring to the classroom. The "funds of knowledge" concept is used to describe the historical accumulation of skills, abilities, bodies of knowledge, life experiences, and worldviews that students from diverse backgrounds bring from home (Hogg, 2011; Rodriguez, 2013). Educators who recognize these assets can apply them in the classroom to enrich all their students' lives. Consider interviewing an ELL to create a "funds of knowledge" inventory. What experiences, relationships, and traditions does the ELL bring from home? How could you incorporate one or more of these family-related or cultural attributes in a lesson? Table 3.1 illustrates an example of a "funds of knowledge" plan designed to strengthen and build on the family-school connection for Yesi, a first-generation Mexican American eighth grade student.

While the languages spoken by English language learners (ELLs) in the United States are diverse, Spanish is the most common language, spoken by 71% of ELLs (Migration Policy Institute, 2015). Data from the U.S. Census Bureau's 2013 American Community Survey (ACS) and the U.S. Department of Education indicates the top three first languages spoken by

Table 3.1 Sample Funds of Knowledge Plan for Yesi, a First-Generation Mexican-American Student

Funds of Knowledge	Home/Community Practices	Classroom Application
Geography	Before coming to the U.S., Yesi's family lived in Puebla, Mexico. Her mom's side of the family is Mexican and French. Her dad's side is Greek, Portuguese, and Spanish.	The class could find Puebla in east-central Mexico on a world map. Students could calculate the distance to Puebla or compare the size and population of Puebla with a large city in our state.
Currency	Yesi's family used pesos while living in Mexico.	One Mexican Peso equals 0.040 U.S. dollar. Students could choose popular items and convert dollars to pesos to compare costs of living here and there.
Agriculture	In Mexico, Yesi's family had a large garden with corn, tomatoes, beans, avocados, lemons, limes, and mangos. They produced dairy products and hominy that was exported to the U.S. for grits.	The class could discuss the main crops and exports of Mexico, and how their climate differs from ours.
Food	Yesi's mother makes posadas, tamales, pozole, and arroz con leche.	Students could research and prepare traditional Mexican dishes. They would need to translate the recipes and convert metric measurements.
Holidays	Americans refer to the Battle of Puebla as *Cinco De Mayo*. Puebla is the only state in Mexico that recognizes *Cinco De Mayo*. Yesi's family also celebrates *Día de los Muertos*, or Day of the Dead.	The class could research the Battle of Puebla. They could also compare holiday traditions and customs from various cultures.
Sports	Yesi's uncle plays recreational soccer and is a huge fan of *Las Chivas de Guadalajara*, a top ranked team in Liga MX, the Mexican football (soccer) league.	The class could research Mexican football teams, stadium locations, famous players, and stats.
Art and Architecture	Puebla is known for its pottery and colonial architecture.	Students could research traditional Mexican art and architecture.

(Cont.)

Table 3.1 Sample Funds of Knowledge Plan for Yesi, a First-Generation Mexican-American Student (Cont.)

Funds of Knowledge	Home/Community Practices	Classroom Application
Music	Yesi's family loves music. Yesi plays the trombone, her sister plays the violin, and her brother plays the French horn.	The class could research Mexican mariachi music, which is prevalent in big tourist cities. Each region of the country has its own version with different instruments. In some areas, Mariachi musicians wear a traditional silver-studded Charro suit and a sombrero. Lively music and dance is performed at quinceañera (girls' 15th birthday celebration).
Language	Yesi's family speaks Spanish in the home. Her grandmother speaks French and Spanish, but does not speak any English.	In language arts, we could utilize Yesi's expertise in Spanish to read texts from different regions of Latin America and compare different Spanish dialects. We could invite Yesi's mom to talk about her experiences in Mexico.

ELLs at the national level are Spanish (71%), Chinese (4%), and Vietnamese (3%).

Spanish is a Romance language that uses the Latin alphabet. Unlike English, the Spanish language uses gendered nouns, two different forms of the verb "to be," fewer pronouns, and fewer prepositions. In addition, word order may not follow the English subject/verb/object pattern; for example, adjectives usually come after the noun, and the indirect object comes before the noun (Benjamin, 2002). The Spanish language also uses more inflection to express different meanings; stressing a particular syllable changes the meaning of a word. Spanish has only five vowel sounds and five diphthongs, as compared to twelve vowel sounds and eight diphthongs in the English language (Migration Policy Institute, 2015). Spanish speakers learning English may have difficulty perceiving and articulating these new sounds. They may also tend to pluralize adjectives, omit pronouns, and confuse the prepositions "in," "on," and "at." They may have difficulty with the possessive apostrophe (Benjamin, 2002) and differences in punctuation.

There are many Chinese dialects, including Mandarin and Cantonese. The English and Chinese languages have significant differences, which can make learning English a serious challenge for Chinese native speakers. The written language uses a symbol to represent a word instead of individual letters, which can make the concept of spelling difficult. In addition, there are many phonemes in the English language, including vowel sounds, which do not exist in Chinese (Frankfurt International School, 2019). Chinese speakers may have difficulty discerning these sounds. Chinese languages do not use verb tense, final consonant sounds, or articles such as "the," "a," or "an." Unlike English, Chinese is a tonal language that uses pitch (the degree of high or low sound) to convey different meanings; thus, the same word could have several different meanings depending on which of the four main tones is used.

Tang (2007) provides a cross-linguistic comparison of Vietnamese and English phonemes (speech-sounds), semantics (word meaning), and grammar. Vietnamese has three types of phonemes—consonants, vowels, and tones. English has more consonant and consonant clusters, while Vietnamese has more single vowels and vowel combinations (Tang, 2007). Five distinct tones are used to convey meaning. The Vietnamese language is monosyllabic, meaning each word is a syllable, while English is multi-syllabic. They do not change verb tense or use forms of the "to be" verb. ELLs may have difficulty understanding the use of prefixes and suffixes; for example, the Vietnamese language does not use the suffix "-er" when making comparisons; instead, the concept of more is expressed using the word for "more" after the adjective (Benjamin, 2002).

In addition to our ELLs, many students come to school speaking variations of English that may not match standard "School English." Unfortunately, many teachers "consistently rank speakers of standardized English as being smarter and of a higher status than speakers of non-standardized English dialects" (Charity-Hudley & Mallinson, 2011, p. 2). White teachers

Table 3.2 Selected Patterns and Features of African American English

Pronunciation	Grammar	Other Features
Absence of the "r" sound	Ain't	Pitch
Variations on the "th" sound	Multiple negatives	Tone
Final consonants "b," "d," and "g"	Forms of "be"	Rhythm
Consonant blends "sk," "nd," "ts," "kt," "sts," "sks"	Past tense	Volume
The "ai" and "oy" sounds	Absence of "-s" inflections	Syllable stress
Vowel mergers		Intonation patterns
The "oo" sound		
The air sound		

(Source: Charity-Hudley & Mallinson, 2011, pp. 69–109)

of African American students, for example, may not understand their students' language variations have systematic, regular rules, conventions, and patterns; their students' "errors" are not simply haphazard or careless mistakes. The African American vernacular style of speaking is "a linguistic difference, not a cognitive or linguistic deficiency" (Charity-Hudley & Mallinson, 2011, p. 102). Selected patterns and features of African American English are found in Table 3.2.

Teachers should be aware that the linguistic "errors" made by their non-standard English speaking students follow specific patterns and are directly related to structural differences between English and the home language. Teachers can use contrastive analysis to raise their students' awareness of the similarities and differences between standard "School English" and African American English. Two poems, *Little Brown Baby* and *Sympathy* by Paul Laurence Dunbar can be used to contrast these linguistic differences. Paul Laurence Dunbar was born in Dayton, Ohio, to parents who had escaped from slavery. His essays and poems have been widely published. Dunbar's work is known for its colorful language, use of dialect, and conversational tone, as well as brilliant rhetorical devices. Paul Laurence Dunbar "sought to show the beauty of both African American English and the style of poetry of the European tradition" (Charity-Hudley & Mallinson, 2011, p. 87). Look for the structural patterns in Dunbar's poems; you may be surprised at how different they are. The poems can be found here:

http://www.poemhunter.com/poem/little-brown-baby/
http://www.poemhunter.com/poem/sympathy/

Regardless of the home language, students who are learning "School English" need opportunities to practice *using* the language, not just listening to it. For these students, working in small groups and collaborating with peers is crucial.

Questions to Consider

1. How might linguistic differences influence school outcomes for students?
2. How can we provide opportunities for ELLs to practice speaking, and not just listening to, English in our classrooms?
3. What strengths do students bring from diverse backgrounds?
4. How could we tap into our students' "funds of knowledge" to strengthen the home-school connection?
5. How can teachers model positive responses to language variations?

Strategies for Teachers

◆ Have lots of books at different reading levels available for students.
◆ Build a class library of children's literature with both English and Spanish versions.
◆ Invite a Spanish speaking student to read aloud a children's book in Spanish, then give the class a "quiz" on the book.
◆ Create teams of two or three students to "tutor" each member of the team in their own language, whatever

it might be. A student from Mexico, for example, could tutor a student from America speaking Spanish, and then switch and the student speaking English could tutor the Mexican student. This levels the playing field.

♦ Create dictionaries using linguistically different languages to identify common objects and terms.

♦ Label objects in the classroom in English, Spanish, and other languages spoken by your students.

♦ Have students analyze text for figurative language, especially idioms which may baffle ELLs.

♦ Think out loud for your students as you work through a math problem or a writing task.

♦ Use fill-in-the-blank lecture notes to simplify note taking.

♦ When notices go home from school, make sure they are written in more than one language. If the majority of your ELLs speak Spanish, make sure the notices are also in Spanish, and French, or whatever different languages are spoken in your school.

References

Benjamin, A. (2002). *Differentiated instruction: A guide for middle and high school teachers*. Larchmont, NY: Eye on Education.

Charity-Hudley, A. H., & Mallinson, C. (2011). *Understanding English language variation in U.S. schools*. New York, NY: Teachers College Press.

Hogg, L. (2011). Funds of knowledge: An investigation of coherence within the literature. *Teaching and Teacher Education, 27*, 666–677.

Frankfurt International School (2019). Language differences. Retrieved from http://esl.fis.edu/grammar/langdiff/index.htm.

Migration Policy Institute (2015). Top languages spoken by English Language Learners nationally and by state. Retrieved from https://www.migrationpolicy.org/research/top-languages-spoken-english-language-learners-nationally-and-state.

Rodriguez, G. (2013). Power and agency in education: Exploring the pedagogical dimensions of funds of knowledge. *Review of Research in Education, 37*(1), 87–120.

Tang, G. (2007). Cross-linguistic analysis of Vietnamese and English with implications for English acquisition and maintenance in the United States. *Journal of Southeast Asian American Education and Advancement, 2*(3), 1–33.

4

Socioeconomic Diversity

Case Study

Mrs. Flynn had been teaching for more than ten years. It was parent-teacher conference day, and she already knew from experience which parents would show up and which ones wouldn't. As usual, she had scheduled the parents' appointments in 15-minute increments during the regular school day hours, and she had sent a note home informing them of their assigned time. Lindsey's parents arrived ten minutes early. With a smile, Mrs. Flynn handed them their child's report card. She thought to herself, "I don't even need to meet with these parents. Lindsey is always on time, turns in her homework and does everything expected of her. Clearly, her parents value her education."

On the other hand, Jimmy displayed some behavior problems, never turned in homework, and had very poor grades, but Mrs. Flynn was sure his parents would not show up. It never occurred to her Jimmy's mother might be working two jobs and unable to make an appointment in the middle of the day. Transportation was difficult for her; furthermore, finding childcare for her other children made parent-teacher conferences challenging to attend.

Had she found alternative ways to communicate with his mother, Mrs. Flynn would have found out the power company had turned off their electricity two months ago, and Jimmy had been struggling to finish his homework in the dark. In addition, he was responsible for taking care of his two younger siblings while his mother was at work. However, Mrs. Flynn just assumed this family did not care about education and made no effort to support Jimmy.

Chapter Content

According to the U.S. Census Bureau (2017), 40.6 million people in the United States live in poverty. In 2016, 19% of all children (14.1 million) in the U.S. lived in poverty, which is about one in every five children. As of 2016, the Federal poverty line was defined as $24,339 for a family of four (Kids Count Data Center, 2017). It is an eye-opening experience to ask middle school students to calculate a monthly budget for housing, utilities, transportation, telephone, food, and childcare; after multiplying this number by 12, the students can compare it to the Federal poverty line.

Numerous studies have documented the effect of poverty on academic achievement. The Education & Workforce Development Task Force (2016) conducted a study "to explain the impact of socioeconomic factors on developing communication skills, learning, academic performance, and school dropouts" (p. 5). They found the traditional financial measures of socioeconomic status, family income and family poverty, were both more highly correlated with proficiency in math and reading standardized tests than with attendance and graduation (p. 13). Another study found "children in the school districts with the highest concentrations of poverty score an average of more than four grade levels below children in the richest districts" (Public Impact, 2018, p. 2). Interestingly, family income is the single most reliable predictor of achievement on the SAT (*source:* http://www .edchange.org/multicultural/quizzes.html).

Although poverty is measured by income, children in socioeconomically challenged families and communities do not only struggle due to lack of financial resources. There are many variables associated with poverty. For example, low parental educational attainment and transportation barriers may keep parents away from the school. Poor nutrition, limited access to health care, and substandard housing exasperate the problem. Financial instability, psychological stress, and the stigma of being poor are factors as well.

One's socioeconomic status has implications across a wide range of social institutions, including schools, health care providers, and banks. Class status is closely related to where one lives, and one's neighborhood schools can be strong or weak depending on the financial resources and tax base of the neighborhood, town, or city. Health care is expensive and associated with full-time employment; the rising cost of health care limits access to poor people. Bank lending practices limit access to housing, transportation, and schools.

One school practice that perpetuates the cycle of poverty is tracking. Presumably, the intent of tracking is to make schools more efficient, but the practice is dangerous and perpetuates the achievement gap for poor children, especially poor children of color. Supporters of tracking claim it is easier to teach homogeneous classes and it allows more "capable" students access to a more rigorous curriculum. This claim is premised on the belief that tracking is fair because with hard work, any student can chart their own path. Yet these paths are not level playing fields. Schools use testing to sort students into groups and assign them to different classes and curricula based on their perceived ability or future potential. However, these tests are biased—children from white, wealthy families consistently test better than poor children of color (English, 2002). As a result, tracking effectively segregates students by race and class.

Jeannie Oakes (2005) has studied tracking for decades. She conducted a large-scale study to analyze the effects of tracking on 13,719 adolescents in 25 schools across the United States. She found poor students and students of color were grossly overrepresented in the lower academic tracks. She also found mobility between tracks was limited; once assigned to a low track, a student was unlikely to move up. Furthermore, tracking did not improve students' self-esteem or academic achievement for anyone. She concluded tracking practices distribute knowledge inequitably, limit opportunities to learn, and socialize students differently (Oakes, 2005).

Tracking has long-term implications. Curricular decisions made for students in middle school can set them up for success or failure in high school and beyond. For example, placement decisions in middle school mathematics classes have powerful ramifications. Because middle school math provides a gateway to the high school's hierarchical structure of mathematics courses, students who take algebra early are much more likely to gain access to advanced mathematics courses during their high school years. Students who do not take algebra in middle school are unlikely to reach calculus. This obstacle has consequences for students' postsecondary outcomes and ultimately limits their career paths and potential earnings.

Recently, middle and high schools have undertaken a broad initiative to enroll fewer students in low-track courses by requiring students to take more challenging ones. This shift is particularly noticeable in mathematics. Domina, Hanselman, Hwang, and McEachin (2016) investigated the state of California's "Algebra-For-All" effort and found the proportion of California eighth-graders enrolled in algebra between 2003 and 2013 nearly doubled to 65%. How did they do it? Some schools "de-tracked" by enrolling all eighth-graders in algebra, while others "tracked up." The schools that "tracked up" moved their lower achieving students to algebra, but they also created new, more-advanced geometry classes for the high-achieving students. Domina et al. (2016) argue that "tracking up" is a strategy by which socially-advantaged groups effectively maintain inequality.

In high-poverty schools, factors that perpetuate achievement gaps include:

◆ Limited resources at the school or district level
◆ Unequal access to excellent teachers, teaching methods, and materials
◆ Teacher bias and low expectations
◆ Rigid tracking with differential access to gifted education and advanced courses
◆ Access to supplemental academic services such as tutoring and music lessons

- ◆ Access to enrichment including books, computers, summer camps, and travel
- ◆ Substandard or crowded housing
- ◆ Changing schools due to housing instability
- ◆ Health and well-being, including food insecurity and sleep quality
- ◆ Mental health, including exposure to violence and trauma

Another problem with tracking identified by research is that young, less experienced teachers are often assigned the lowest tracks; expectations for this group of students are often much lower, thus the students live down to the teacher's expectations of them. Because curriculum in the lower tracks may often be dull with little connection to students' real lives, they become bored and often discover yet another reason to tune out. What is the motivation to succeed when you have been relegated to the bottom? It can be a difficult situation dealing with yet another label, especially in middle schools where students struggle to find their identity.

Recently the COVID-19 pandemic has exposed and exasperated deep inequities in our society. With respect to today's remote learning environment, teachers must be aware of and respectful of students' differences and privacy concerns as we deal more and more with Zoom video calls and asynchronous learning. Virtual learning is particularly challenging for students living in poverty. These students are less likely to have the technology and tools they need to successfully navigate online learning from home. Even if they have a school-issued device, students who live in poor rural areas may not have access to a reliable Internet connection. Some students may have the technology and the access, but do not want to have their video on for virtual meetings like Zoom. Perhaps they don't want to show they're watching younger siblings while a parent/caregiver is away, or they don't want people to see their home. This difference in availability of learning resources may stigmatize students, and ultimately widen the achievement gap.

Many well-meaning efforts aimed at addressing the achievement gap are focused on deficits in children. Some of these efforts are premised on the view that students are not motivated or are not trying hard enough. Lack of success is blamed on a group culture that does not value learning. How can we change the narrative that blames the victim? We argue the focus should shift from blaming the students to taking a hard look at the schools themselves and the decisions around tracking, hiring practices, investment in infrastructure, discipline, and many other choices that teachers and administrators make every day (Public Impact, 2018). Think about it—if we find a dead fish in a pond, we tend to focus on what was wrong with the fish. Too often, we fail to ask what is wrong with the water.

Questions to Consider

1. How might poverty impact student achievement?
2. What assumptions might be harmful to make about students living in poverty?
3. How can teachers challenge and support students who have limited resources at home?
4. How can teachers find accessible ways to make home-school connections?
5. What are the long-term effects of tracking and how does it perpetuate the cycle of poverty?

Strategies for Teachers

◆ Provide a safe, structured environment with clear boundaries, predictable routines, and a positive classroom culture.
◆ Use proactive classroom management and explicitly teach expected behaviors.
◆ Use a restorative approach to discipline as opposed to a punitive approach.
◆ Treat all students with respect.

- Take the time to get to know each student and his/her living conditions.
- Watch for signs of traumatic stress including fear, exhaustion, and aggression.
- Have high expectations for all students, and then provide the tools needed to achieve those expectations.
- Be sure any resources necessary for classroom activities are available for all students.
- Send home any necessary materials for assigned projects.
- Be sensitive to unattainable homework tasks. For example, instead of assigning students to measure the area of their driveway, have them measure the ceiling tiles in your classroom. Not all students will have a driveway.
- Expose students to the arts by visiting museums, attending performances, or taking field trips.
- Work with the school guidance counselor to refer families for services such as food banks and Secret Santa.

References

Domina, T., Hanselman, P., Hwang, N., & McEachin, A. (2016). Detracking and tracking up mathematics course placements in California middle schools, 2003–2013. *American Educational Research Journal, 53*(4), 1229–1266.

Education & Workforce Development Task Force (2016). The impact of poverty on a child's academic performance. The Institute for Public Policy & Economic Development at Wilkes University. Retrieved from http://docplayer.net/26957215-The-impact-of-poverty-on-a-child-s-academic-performance.html

English, F. (2002). On the intractability of the achievement gap in urban schools and the discursive practice of continuing racial discrimination. *Education and Urban Society, 34*, 298–311.

Kids Count Data Center (2017). A project of the Annie E. Casey Foundation. Retrieved from http://datacenter.kidscount.org/.

Oakes, J. (2005). *Keeping track: How schools structure inequality* (2nd ed.). New Haven, CT: Yale University Press.

Public Impact (2018). *Closing achievement gaps in diverse and low-poverty schools: An action guide for district leaders.* Chapel Hill, NC: Public Impact and Geneva, Switzerland: Oak Foundation. Retrieved from http://publicimpact.com/pi/wp-content/uploads/2018/08/Closing_Achievement_Gaps_in_Diverse_and_Low-Poverty_Schools.pdf.

U.S. Census Bureau (2017). Income and poverty in the United States: 2016. Report Number: P60-259. Retrieved from https://www.census.gov/library/publications/2017/demo/p60-259.html.

5

Family Structures

Case Study

Erica had never known her father. She lived with her mother and her grandmother in a one-bedroom apartment. Her mother worked two jobs to support the family. Every morning Erica got up at 5:00 am and did her chores before riding the bus to school. Unless she had basketball practice, she attended a neighborhood afterschool program where she helped younger students with their homework. Every evening she ate dinner and watched TV with her grandmother, but only after her homework was done. Her mother and grandmother were very strict and would not let her stay out late. "Nothing good happens on the street after dark," they would say. "You get yourself home and stay out of trouble."

Erica made good grades at school, but she did not particularly like it. Her teachers were kind, but did not seem to expect much from her. She was really good at math and wanted to take Honors pre-algebra, but couldn't find a teacher willing to nominate her. She was bored and tended to sit in the back of the room by herself.

One day Erica's math teacher asked her to stay after school. She was excited and hopeful that Mr. Green had finally noticed her ability and her good grades in mathematics. He asked her to sit down. "Erica, would you be interested in participating in the school's new mentoring program?" he asked.

"Yes!" she said at once. "I am already tutoring some of the kids in my neighborhood. I would be happy to participate!"

"This program is to help you," he continued. "It's a very good opportunity for a girl like you."

Erica took a deep breath. "A girl like me? Mr. Green, why did you select me for this program?"

Mr. Green would not meet her eyes. "This program is designed to help students from single parent homes who are at risk for dropping out of school. We believe you would benefit from having someone who cares about you and cares about your success in school."

"But I do have people who care about me and my success in school," Erica said. "Why would you think I don't?"

Chapter Content

The percentage of families where both parents work has increased tenfold. The number of one-parent families, whether single mother or single father, continues to rise. Perhaps there has been a death or a divorce in the family. Or perhaps there never has been a second parent in the family. Young adolescents who decide the separation and divorce are their fault and vow to bring their parents back together feel even more disappointment, more despair, and more stress when their attempts fail. What about students who live in a car or a homeless shelter? Recent research also documents the number of children being raised by their grandparents, with no parent present, as another recent phenomenon. The security of a family is no longer guaranteed. Yet middle-level students need this support just as much as younger children and perhaps even more.

At the same time, it is important for teachers not to make assumptions about a student's family. The lack of a father in the home does not guarantee the child is "at risk." Take the time to get to know each student's family situation before declaring it to be deficient.

What about the family with transracially adopted children? Does that create a social problem for these young people because they are different from the rest of their classmates, and also, from their immediate family members? One African American female, who was interviewed when she was in her twenties, reported she was adopted by a loving and large Irish American family when she was very young. The family lived in what she called a "lily white" community. She stated that all through her middle school and high school years, she never once was invited to a school dance or a prom. She was "too black" for the white community and "too white" for the African American community. Although her adopted mother told her it would be better once she was in college, it did not happen either. It was the same predicament. Did this affect her? You bet! Does it affect her still? You bet! Could anything have been done to alleviate this situation? With a rising number of transracially adopted children, this is a question with which adoptive parents will continue to struggle—how to provide well-rounded, accepting, and successful lives for their children.

Another transracial child was adopted from an orphanage in Korea when he was a seven-year-old. His adoptive parents reported he had all the food, clothing, and toys he needed, but no physical bonding. As he grew into his young adolescent years, he still had not achieved the social skills necessary to be successful. Only after attending an alternative school and receiving hours and hours of therapy did he begin to adjust and gain the social skills he so sorely needed. When talking with this young man, it is apparent the depth to which these experiences affected him during his middle school years. Was this young man interested in math or science? Not really. He was interested in how he could "fit in" and be like the rest of his peers. It takes a lot of caring and concern not only on the part of the parents, but also from teachers, guidance counselors, and administration to seek out these students and find a way to help them become successful young adults.

A prevailing myth of early adolescence is that 10- to 15-year-olds increasingly turn to their peers for guidance. While young adolescents do need greater autonomy, they do not need or want a complete break with their parents and families. Parents need opportunities to make meaningful decisions on issues and problems concerning their children's education. In order to keep parents informed, teachers cannot rely on young adolescents to transmit important information. How many times have teachers insisted on a cleanout time for backpacks and found notices and reminders in May of events which happened back in October? Find ways to inform parents of what is going on in your schools. In order to offer families opportunities to support learning at home and at school, one school district in Alabama invites parents into classes, with parents learning right along with students.

What one family expects of a son or daughter can be totally opposite from what another family might expect. Many times, parents remember what it was like for them when they were in a middle-level school, and this is not what they want for their children. If parents attended a traditional, departmentalized junior high school, and now their young adolescents come home talking about interdisciplinary units, saying they don't go to math class, but do a lot of math in English class, parents are apt to be upset. If parents of a highly intelligent child discover their young adolescent is participating in cooperative learning activities with students of all abilities working together, many parents will assume their child is being cheated. Some parents believe their young adolescent should learn with students of the same ability. They disregard the fact that by working with students of other abilities, high-achieving students also learn through social interaction and opportunities to hear and work through the different thought processes of many other students.

A great many families are willing to work closely with teachers for the good of their children. They are the parents who always attend parent conferences, volunteer whenever possible as chaperones, and check to be sure their children bring home and finish their homework. Those parents are willing to get involved in their child's education; more school districts must find ways to get more parents to this level. However, we must also find novel ways to involve those families who may not be able to volunteer or visit the school. For example, a South Carolina middle school found a low-tech, but meaningful way to involve families through an informal homework assignment. Middle school students were asked to survey every family member at home and list all of their favorite foods. The class data was then compiled at school, categorized by food groups, entered into an Excel spreadsheet, and displayed using various types of graphs.

Parents should never be placed in the middle between teachers and students. We plan parent and teacher conferences and complain because parents do not attend, even though the conferences are scheduled during the day when most parents work. We must find a way to be more flexible if we want parents involved with their youngsters. One middle school made sure at least two of the scheduled parent-teacher conferences were on a Thursday night and a Saturday morning because of parents' work schedules. An additional dilemma arises when parents arrive for a scheduled appointment only to be faced with a table of five to eight persons who appear ready to "do battle." In such a situation, parents tend to either "fold" or become defensive. One parent suggested teachers remember what it is like going into a doctor's office, not knowing what, if anything, is wrong, and then not understanding the terminology used to explain the ailment. When talking with parents, teachers must forget the jargon when discussing students and their needs. Even as some parents are terrified of attending parent conferences, some teachers are terrified of communicating with parents. Many teachers worry that if parents are invited to participate in curriculum planning, they will somehow take over and demand a return to what and how they were taught when they were in junior high school. By involving parents as partners in the education of middle-level students, the goals for our students will be reached—successful students who are also lifelong learners.

The transition to virtual learning during the recent COVID-19 pandemic has blurred the boundaries between school and home. When we require our students to participate in online class meetings such as Zoom with their cameras on, we are inviting ourselves into their homes without their permission. For some, this intrusion into the family's private space may be uncomfortable or even a source of embarrassment. Consider the student who does not want others to know her family's socioeconomic status.

Perhaps a student's household is noisy, crowded, and chaotic. What about the student who is living in a homeless shelter? Allowing teachers and classmates to peer into this most intimate space may cause young adolescents to feel exposed, vulnerable, and judged. Teachers need to be mindful of families' privacy and find ways to engage their students without requiring them to turn on the camera.

Questions to Consider

1. How might family background and home environment affect student learning and performance?
2. What assumptions might be harmful to make about students living in non-traditional families?
3. What strengths, relationships, and traditions do children bring from home to school?
4. How can we promote family involvement and strengthen the family-school connection?

Strategies for Teachers

◆ Do not assume there is a mother and father living in the home. It may be a one-parent family, or children being raised by grandparents.

◆ Open communication between parents and the school by sending frequent newsletters to parents. Newsletters should be available in languages of all students. Teachers might consider using the Remind App, a free text messaging app which can be translated into 90 different languages.

◆ Find accessible and meaningful ways to involve families in homework. For example, students could interview an older family member for an oral history project, bring in a family recipe, or survey family members to collect data.

◆ Invite parents into the school for informal chats over tea or during special programs.

◆ Avoid "educationese." Explain concepts such as inter-disciplinary teams, advisory, and portfolios in simple, straightforward language.

◆ Treat all parents with respect.

◆ Show appreciation for parental support and volun-teerism. Look for opportunities to involve parents who are unable to be present during school hours. Recognize those parents who have supported and volunteered for school activities and field trips, as well as those who pro-vide support in alternate ways.

◆ Initiate student-led parent-teacher conferences. A mid-dle school in Colorado asked students to create portfo-lios beginning in the sixth-grade. Each spring students would invite their parents, aunts, uncles, siblings, or grandparents and present, along with one of their teach-ers, samples illustrating their work in the last year. By the time students finished eighth-grade, there was ample evi-dence of their progress, learning, and readiness to enter high school.

◆ Establish a parent-teacher group. These groups are a great help in letting the community at large know what is happening in the local middle school.

◆ Make the school Web page accessible to parents. Some families will not have access to the Internet and will need special consideration if information is available only on school Web pages.

◆ Provide evening or weekend appointments for parent-teacher conferences. With more and more families hav-ing both parents working and with more single parent families, it is important to schedule evening or weekend parent-teacher appointments.

◆ Do not insist on your class doing a family tree.

6

Physical Diversity

Case Study

Melissa Price was a very bright, very quiet child. She was a talented writer and a gifted artist. She always sat in the front of the room and gave the teacher her full, undivided attention. One day Mrs. Arthur gave the class a set of verbal instructions while writing a homework assignment on the board. With her back turned to the students, she instructed them to sit in a specific area during the upcoming pep rally. Later in the afternoon, she was quite surprised to see Melissa walk across the gym to sit with a friend on the opposite side. "You obviously weren't paying attention in class," she told the student, as she moved her and assigned three days of lunch detention.

A few weeks later Melissa's parents met with Mrs. Arthur on parent-teacher conference day. "Your daughter is an outstanding student," the teacher said. "And she is so well behaved. I still can't believe she deliberately disobeyed my instructions regarding the pep rally."

"Is it possible Melissa didn't understand your instructions?" her mother asked.

"I was very clear," Mrs. Arthur responded. "I asked them all to sit with me near the scoreboard. They were told not to go sit with their friends."

"Could Melissa see your face when you gave those instructions?" Mrs. Price gently asked. "You see, my daughter has an auditory processing problem and has to have visual cues in order to understand. For all intents and purposes, she is deaf. She needs to be able to read your lips."

"Well, I had turned to write on the board. But... I didn't know!" Mrs. Arthur said, clearly upset. "Why didn't she tell me?"

"She didn't want you to know," Melissa's mother said. "She doesn't like to draw attention to the fact she's different. She preferred to just take the detention."

Chapter Content

Have you ever thought about what it would be like to have a student with a hearing impairment or auditory processing disorder? How would you need to adjust your teaching to help a student who is blind or has low vision? What accommodations would a student with a physical disability need in order to be successful? Aside from their disability, what strengths and abilities might the student have? How would you challenge and support that student?

We argue that teachers can approach physical disabilities and impairments from an attribute perspective as opposed to a deficit perspective by using brain-based and research-based strategies to differentiate curriculum. For example, accommodations for hearing impaired students may include using a computer with talk-to-text capability and videos with closed captioning. Accommodations for visually impaired students can provide access to instructional materials through tactile or auditory senses, books on tape, and oral testing. Visual accommodations may include enlarging print materials, increasing the contrast and clarity of print materials, and decreasing glare and visual clutter to make items easier to view. Tactile accommodations may include using maps, graphs, and diagrams with raised lines or dots, using three-dimensional models, and providing hands-on experiences with real objects instead of pictures.

In addition to providing auditory, visual, and tactile accommodations, we recommend all middle school teachers provide opportunities for active engagement through kinesthetic learning (Lengel & Kuczala, 2010). We define kinesthetic learning as an instructional strategy that connects physical movement and social interaction with academic content. The goal is to get students actively engaged and "learning by doing" as they investigate concepts through physical movement. This is particularly important for young adolescents.

We know adolescence is a critical time for physical development. Middle school educators who understand the developmental uniqueness of this age group seek to provide "intellectually engaging learning activities, socially engaging learning activities, and physically engaging learning activities" (Edwards, 2016, p. 32). Regular physical activity in children and adolescents promotes health and fitness. Movement increases the heart rate and stimulates brain function, which facilitates a child's ability to learn. Physical activity promotes biological changes in the brain which increase neural cells and connections (Reilly, Burkist, & Gross, 2012). The U.S. Department of Health and Human Services (2018) advocates physical activity for brain health. Regular physical activity "results in improved cognition, including performance on academic achievement tests, executive function, processing speed, and memory" (p. 40) as well as a reduced risk of depression.

Numerous studies support the conclusion that physical activity has a positive influence on memory, concentration, and classroom behavior (Reilly, Burkist, & Gross, 2012). Grissom (2005) found a statistically significant positive correlation between fitness and standardized test scores in math. Furthermore, students who were more physically fit had fewer absences and fewer disciplinary referrals. The findings "remained significant while controlling for gender, race, and socioeconomic status" (Blom, Alvarez, Zhang, & Kolbo, 2011, p. 13). The cognitive benefits of physical activity apply to all students, including those with conditions such as attention-deficit/ hyperactivity disorder (ADHD) (Zeigler, 2011).

With regard to physical characteristics, diversity is easy to see every time one walks down a middle school hallway, looks across the athletic field, or watches students rushing to the bus at the end of the school day. Young adolescent males range from short and stout, to tall, skinny, and clumsy, from boys to young men whose muscles are fully developed. Young adolescent females also range from the small girl who carries a teddy bear and is still a child, to the young woman who is fully developed with breasts, hips, a waist, and acne, and who wonders what to do with and how to take care of all these new "attachments." Of course, there are many students who don't fit either description and wonder if they ever will.

Girls typically reach puberty about two years before boys, but both experience a significant growth spurt with marked height and weight gains. Van Hoose, Strahan, and L'Esperance (2009) remind us young adolescents gain an average of 10–20 inches in height and 40–50 pounds in weight between ages 10 and 15. As adults, we view this as a natural phenomenon, but young adolescents often worry that something may be wrong with them because of these significant physical changes. Each certainly affects how they feel about themselves. If they are bigger or smaller, shorter or taller than what they perceive to be the norm, young adolescents tend to think there is something wrong with them. If they deviate from the norm, then they think they are abnormal. Middle grades students spend a lot of time worrying about their physical differences—at home, and at school during classes (p. 10).

Because the extremities—hands, feet, ears—grow more quickly than other parts of the body, young adolescents are often seen, and in reality feel clumsy, with shoes the size of "gunboats" and hands that knock over everything. It is not surprising that our students feel like their bodies have been invaded by aliens.

Here is an example of what NOT to do when dealing with middle-level students. A principal addressed the student body at the beginning of the school year, stressing the differences among students. Unexpectedly, he called two young ladies to the stage, one quite fully developed and one who was still "waiting." Standing them back to back and locking their arms together, he declared this an example of the differences between peers! To even begin to acknowledge the multitude of feelings in the minds of those two young women is unthinkable! Embarrassed? Confused? Distressed? Mortified?

Downright angry? Any or all of these feelings might have been a part of that terrible moment, and deservedly so. Whatever would possess an administrator to conduct this display of arrogance? Not thinking? Not an excuse. An episode of this nature should never happen in any school.

It is very important for middle-level teachers to remember these physical differences when planning classroom activities. It is important during gym class, for example, when captains choose teams from their classmates. This situation leaves the non-athletic, over- or underweight student waiting to be the last one chosen while his or her self-esteem and self-concept take a nose dive. It is also important to remember when deciding whether to use standard desks and chairs in the classroom, where the fully developed young man mentioned earlier is picking up the desk with his knees, bouncing it around, trying to find a way to get comfortable while staying focused on learning. Middle-level students would much rather be involved in hands-on, active learning than simply sitting in a desk which is too small in the first place. Is it any wonder students find the slightest excuse to leap out of their seats to sharpen a pencil—regardless if it is in the middle of something important?

When asked how he handled diversity in his classroom, one teacher responded, "We don't have any diversity in my classroom. We're all alike." Perhaps students are all of the same socioeconomic status, or perhaps they are all males or all females, but this teacher was mistaken: there are multifaceted and nuanced aspects of diversity in every classroom, especially in middle school. Ignoring those differences will result in misunderstood young adolescents.

Questions to Consider

1. Why is it important for teachers to avoid drawing attention to or comparing physical characteristics of young adolescents?
2. How could you limit the amount of time students spend sitting and listening?

3. Why is it particularly important for adolescents to have opportunities to move?
4. How might your students use their hands and bodies as tools for learning?
5. What accommodations might you need to make for a student with a visual impairment?
6. What accommodations might you need to make for a student with a hearing impairment?
7. What accommodations might you need to make for a student with attention deficit disorder (ADD) or ADHD?
8. What accommodations might you need to make for a student with an orthopedic physical disability?

Strategies for Teachers

◆ Rapid, uneven growth can result in physical discomfort, restlessness, and the need for movement. Offer frequent opportunities to stand up, stretch, and move around the classroom.

◆ Over the course of one week, jot down 1) what the teacher is doing and 2) what the students are doing. Who is more active?

◆ Periodically ask students to stand up, turn and talk to a partner for 60 seconds, and then sit back down.

◆ Incorporate kinesthetic activities to teach concepts. Students can use their bodies to model, role-play, or walk through numerous structures, functions, and processes.

◆ Invite students to dramatize mathematics concepts such as plotting points on a Cartesian coordinate system using their bodies on a *Twister* mat. Other kinesthetic math activities might include using arms to model acute, obtuse, and right angles; acting out operations on a number line; teaching translations, rotations, and reflections by dancing *The Electric Slide*; and constructing a human graph.

◆ Engage your students in kinesthetic activities to explore science concepts. For example, students could role-play molecules in a solid, liquid, and gas; perform the functions of organelles in a cell; walk through the processes of the rock cycle; and simulate astronomical movements such as rotation, revolution, and seasons.

◆ Set up a simulated crime scene investigation with stations. Students must solve a problem or collect evidence as they rotate through stations around the room to solve the crime.

◆ Ask students to line up by birthdays or initials of their last names, not by height, shoe size, or other potentially embarrassing physical characteristics.

◆ Launch a lesson using tactile objects such as feathers, foam, or plant material.

◆ Be sure to provide both visual and auditory cues. Some students may have difficulty processing information in one modality.

◆ Changes in sleep patterns often occur in adolescence, which may cause students to have difficulty waking up in the morning. If possible, have a flexible schedule to accommodate students who have difficulty waking up in the morning.

◆ If a student is overweight and having difficulty fitting into a classroom seat, quietly make other arrangements without drawing attention.

◆ When reading aloud in class, do not insist on someone with a speaking difficulty (for example, a lisp or stutter) to read aloud and be embarrassed.

◆ Many times middle school students will go with a parent or friend on errands. Ask students to investigate a downtown area for handicapped access for those who are blind, use wheelchairs, or are hearing impaired. For example, how easy is it to enter the post office or bank when on crutches or in a wheelchair? Does the automatic door open outward, thereby making it impossible for a person in a wheelchair to enter? Do crossing lights flash for those hard of hearing, or ring for those who have difficulty seeing?

References

Blom, L., Alvarez, J., Zhang, L., & Kolbo, J. (2011). Associations between health-related physical fitness, academic achievement and selected academic behaviors of elementary and middle school students in the state of Mississippi. *ICHPER-SD Journal of Research, 6*(1), 13–19.

Edwards, S. (2016). *Active learning in the middle grades classroom.* Westerville, OH: Association for Middle Level Education.

Grissom, J. B. (2005). Physical fitness and academic achievement. *Journal of Exercise Physiology, 8,* 11–25.

Lengel, T., & Kuczala, M. (2010). *The kinesthetic classroom: Teaching and learning through movement.* Thousand Oaks, CA: Corwin-A SAGE Company.

Reilly, E., Burkist, C., & Gross, M. K. (2012). Movement in the classroom: Boosting brain power, fighting obesity. *Kappa Delta Pi Record, 48*(2), 62–66.

U.S. Department of Health and Human Services (2018). *Physical activity guidelines for Americans* (2nd ed.). Washington, DC. Retrieved from https://health.gov/paguidelines/second-edition/pdf/Physical_Activity_Guidelines_2nd_edition.pdf.

Van Hoose, J., Strahan, D., & L'Esperance, M. (2009). *Promoting harmony: Young adolescent development and school practices* (3rd ed.). Westerville, OH: National Middle School Association.

Zeigler, C. A. (2011). *Teaching teens with ADD, ADHD, & executive function deficits* (2nd ed.). Bethesda, MD: Woodbine House.

7

Gender and Sexual Diversity

Case Study

As a first-year teacher, Ms. Parker was anxious to learn her eighth-grade students' names in order to connect with them on a personal level. On the first day of class, she called the roll aloud and asked each student if she was pronouncing their name correctly. During her third period science class, she called out the name "Michael Rasmussen." There was a pause, and then a student quietly murmured a response from the very back of the room. "Do you go by Michael?" Ms. Parker cheerfully inquired, still looking at the roster. "Or do you prefer to be called Mike?" Then she looked up. She was quite surprised to see that the student named Michael had stylish purple hair, long red fingernails, and flawless makeup. There was an awkward silence. "Oh," said Ms. Parker. "So do you go by Michaela then?" Row after row of students turned around to stare at Michael, who now looked extremely uncomfortable. Ms. Parker did not know what to say. She hurriedly returned her attention to the roster and finished the list.

The next day, at the end of the class period, Michael came forward and asked to speak to Ms. Parker privately. The student explained although her birth name was Michael, she would prefer to be called Kayla. She had just moved to the area and was in the process of transitioning from male to female. "Please, Ms. Parker," the student asked, "would you please call me

Kayla? I really don't want my classmates to know my birth name." Even though her parents had requested it, the school had refused to change the student's legal name on their records.

"Of course I will, Kayla," asked Ms. Parker, "but I have a question. When I refer to you in class, should I use the pronouns she and her?" "Yes!" exclaimed Kayla. "Thank you. You are the only teacher who has cared enough to ask."

Chapter Content

Gender diversity in middle school classrooms is just as complex and involved as gender diversity in any other setting. First, let's clarify the difference between sex and gender. Sex is the biological status of being male or female as determined at birth. Biological sex is based on internal and external physical characteristics including chromosomes and genitalia. Gender, on the other hand, is a social construct. We are taught from an early age that blue is for boys and pink is for girls. We are socialized to believe boys are tough and strong, while girls are nurturing and pretty. We tend to think of gender as either/or, in binary terms, but it isn't that simple.

Gender identity refers to an individual's self-concept as masculine, feminine, both, neither, or somewhere in between. Gender identity may or may not correspond to one's assignment at birth. People who do experience congruency between assignment at birth and their gendered sense of self are known as cisgender. "Cis" in cisgender translates to "on this side" in Latin, while "trans," as in transgender, means "on the other side." Some individuals who identify as transgender begin a process of transition to living as the gender with which they identify, rather than the sex assigned to them at birth (Human Rights Campaign, 2020). Transitioning may include a change in appearance, selection of a new name, and a request that people use their preferred pronouns. Sometimes, transitioning includes hormone therapy or surgery.

There are continuums of gender identity, gender expression, and sexual orientation. The term genderqueer includes individuals who do not identify as a man or as a woman, or who identify as both, or who identify outside the gender binary. Other gender identity terms include agender, androgynous, bigender, demigender, genderfluid/flux, and questioning. Gender expression refers to the ways in which an individual communicates their gender identity through appearance and behavior. Gender expression may or may not conform to society's gender norms and expectations.

Sexual orientation may or may not align with an individual's gender identity. Sexual orientation refers to a person's emotional and sexual attraction to other people. A person may identify their sexual orientation as heterosexual, lesbian, gay, bisexual, pansexual, demisexual, fluid, queer, or questioning. The term pansexuality refers to the sexual or romantic attraction of one person to another regardless of their biological sex, gender identity, or sexual orientation. Demisexuality is a sexual orientation in which an individual only experiences sexual attraction after making a strong emotional connection with a specific person.

It is important to understand sexual orientation and gender identity are two different things. At a time when all young adolescents try to figure out who they are and what they will become, the added pressure from questions about their sexual orientation is even more confusing. Where and to whom do they turn to ask questions? To parents who may refuse to acknowledge their dilemma or, in a worst-case scenario, kick them out of the house? To teachers who, many times, are afraid to even discuss non-conforming gender and sexuality issues for fear of losing their jobs? To the guidance counselor who may, unfortunately, tell the student, "It's okay. You'll grow out of it." It is important students know how to find the information they need, when they need it. This is a fact of life and will not be solved by refusing to discuss such contentious issues. The Human Rights Campaign (2020) offers the following glossary of terms (Table 7.1) which may be helpful:

Unfortunately, many non-binary youth experience heartbreaking levels of stress, anxiety, rejection, and fear in school. In their 2017 *National School Climate Survey* report, the Gay, Lesbian & Straight Education Network (GLSEN) (2019) surveyed more than

Table 7.1 Glossary of Gender Terms

Ally—A person who is not lesbian, gay, bisexual, transgender, queer, or questioning (LGBTQ) but shows support for LGBTQ people and promotes equality in a variety of ways.

Androgynous—Identifying and/or presenting as neither distinguishably masculine nor feminine.

Asexual—The lack of a sexual attraction or desire for other people.

Biphobia—Prejudice, fear or hatred directed toward bisexual people.

Bisexual—A person emotionally, romantically or sexually attracted to more than one sex, gender or gender identity though not necessarily simultaneously, in the same way or to the same degree.

Cisgender—A term used to describe a person whose gender identity aligns with the sex assigned to them at birth.

Closeted—Describes an LGBTQ person who has not disclosed their sexual orientation or gender identity.

Coming out—The process in which a person first acknowledges, accepts and appreciates their sexual orientation or gender identity and begins to share that with others.

Gay—A person who is emotionally, romantically, or sexually attracted to members of the same gender.

Gender dysphoria—Clinically significant distress caused when a person's assigned birth gender is not the same as the one with which they identify. According to the American Psychiatric Association's Diagnostic and Statistical Manual of Mental Disorders (DSM), the term—which replaces Gender Identity Disorder—"is intended to better characterize the experiences of affected children, adolescents, and adults."

Gender-expansive—Conveys a wider, more flexible range of gender identity and/or expression than typically associated with the binary gender system.

Gender expression—External appearance of one's gender identity, usually expressed through behavior, clothing, haircut or voice, and which may or may not conform to socially defined behaviors and characteristics typically associated with being either masculine or feminine.

Gender-fluid—A person who does not identify with a single fixed gender; of or relating to a person having or expressing a fluid or unfixed gender identity.

Gender identity—One's innermost concept of self as male, female, a blend of both, or neither—how individuals perceive themselves and what they call themselves. One's gender identity can be the same or different from one's sex assigned at birth.

Gender non-conforming—A broad term referring to people who do not behave in a way that conforms to the traditional expectations of their gender, or whose gender expression does not fit neatly into a category.

Genderqueer—Genderqueer people typically reject notions of static categories of gender and embrace a fluidity of gender identity and often, though not always, sexual orientation. People who identify as "genderqueer" may see themselves as being both male and female, neither male nor female, or as falling completely outside these categories.

Table 7.1 Glossary of Gender Terms (Cont.)

Gender transition—The process by which some people strive to more closely align their internal knowledge of gender with its outward appearance. Some people choose to transition; they might begin dressing, using names and pronouns, and/or be socially recognized as another gender. Others undergo physical transitions in which they modify their bodies through medical interventions.

Homophobia—The fear and hatred of, or discomfort with, people who are attracted to members of the same sex.

Intersex—An umbrella term used to describe a wide range of natural bodily variations. In some cases, these traits are visible at birth, and in others, they are not apparent until puberty. Some chromosomal variations of this type may not be physically apparent at all.

Lesbian—A woman who is emotionally, romantically, or sexually attracted to other women.

LGBTQ—An acronym for "lesbian, gay, bisexual, transgender, and queer (or questioning)."

Non-binary—An adjective describing a person who does not identify exclusively as a man or a woman. Non-binary people may identify as being both a man and a woman, somewhere in between, or as falling completely outside these categories. While many also identify as transgender, not all non-binary people do.

Outing—Exposing someone's lesbian, gay, bisexual, or transgender identity to others without their permission. Outing someone can have serious repercussions on employment, economic stability, personal safety, or family situations.

Pansexual—Describes someone who has the potential for emotional, romantic, or sexual attraction to people of any gender though not necessarily simultaneously, in the same way or to the same degree.

Queer—A term people often use to express fluid identities and orientations; often used interchangeably with "LGBTQ."

Questioning—A term used to describe people who are in the process of exploring their sexual orientation or gender identity.

Same-gender loving—A term some prefer to use instead of lesbian, gay, or bisexual to express attraction to and love of people of the same gender.

Sex assigned at birth—The sex (male or female) given to a child at birth, most often based on the child's external anatomy. This is also referred to as "assigned sex at birth."

Sexual orientation—An inherent or immutable enduring emotional, romantic, or sexual attraction to other people.

Transgender—An umbrella term for people whose gender identity and/or expression is different from cultural expectations based on the sex they were assigned at birth. Being transgender does not imply any specific sexual orientation; therefore, transgender people may identify as straight, gay, lesbian, bisexual, etc.

Transphobia—The fear and hatred of, or discomfort with, transgender people.

(Source: https://www.hrc.org/resources/glossary-of-terms)

23,000 adolescents to document the prevalence of anti-LGBTQ language, harassment, and assault in schools. The survey, which has been conducted every two years since 1999, examines school policies and practices and the negative impacts on LGBTQ students' mental health, self-esteem, and educational outcomes. Kosciw, Greytak, Zongrone, Clark, and Truong (2018) found 92.6% of transgender and gender non-conforming (trans/GNC) students reported depression, anxiety, or stress resulting from a negative school climate. Nearly 60% (59.5%) of LGBTQ students said they experience school as a hostile environment. The *National School Climate Survey* found 70.1% of LGBTQ students heard homophobic remarks frequently or often; 36.7% of LGBTQ students were physically harassed (e.g., pushed or shoved) in the past year because of their sexual orientation or gender expression; and 12.4% had been physically assaulted. In addition, nearly half (48.7%) of LGBTQ students reported being victims of cyberbullying; these students reported being harassed or threatened by peers via electronic media, including text messages, emails, or postings on social media in the past year. It's no wonder these students feel uncomfortable, unwelcome, and unsafe at school.

The Human Rights Campaign Foundation (2020) recently conducted a similar survey. Their 2018 LGBTQ Youth Report findings include the following:

♦ 73% of LGBTQ youth have experienced verbal threats because of their actual or perceived LGBTQ identity
♦ 70% have been bullied at school because of their sexual orientation
♦ 77% of LGBTQ youth report receiving unwanted sexual comments, jokes, and gestures in the past year
♦ 11% of LGBTQ youth report they have been sexually attacked or raped because of their actual or assumed LGBTQ identity
♦ 95% report they have trouble getting to sleep at night

Administrators, teachers, and school counselors need to be aware of how pervasive LGBTQ harassment and violence has been—and continues to be—in schools. The Gay, Lesbian &

Straight Education Network reviewed *National School Climate* survey data from 2001 to 2017 and concluded "it is evident that school climate remains quite hostile for many LGBTQ students" (Kosciw et al., 2018, p. xxiv).

Indicators of a negative school climate include hearing biased or homophobic remarks in school; experiencing harassment, rejection, bullying, and isolation; and experiencing discriminatory policies and practices at school (Table 7.2). These negative school experiences have damaging consequences for transgender and gender-expansive youth, and further contribute to hostile learning environments where they feel unsafe and unprotected. This can have a major impact on their overall well-being, with serious implications for mental health. According to the 2010 National Transgender Discrimination Survey, "41% of transgender people had attempted suicide. That number rose to 51% for those who

Table 7.2 Examples of Discriminatory School Policies and Practices Based on Gender

Name	◆ Students are prevented from using their chosen name
	◆ Students are prevented from using their chosen pronouns
Harassment, bullying, and assault	◆ The use of biased language or homophobic remarks
	◆ Unwanted sexual comments, jokes, and gestures
	◆ Verbal harassment
	◆ Verbal threats
	◆ Cyberbullying
	◆ Physical harassment (e.g., pushed, touched)
	◆ Physical assault (e.g., hit, kicked, or attacked)
Bathroom and locker room	◆ Students are required to use the bathroom of their legal sex
	◆ Students are required to use the locker room of their legal sex
Clothing	◆ Students are required to wear gendered attire for graduation, such as different-colored robes for boys and girls
	◆ Students are required to wear gendered attire for official school photographs or events (e.g., girls wearing dresses and boys wearing neckties)
	◆ Students are required to wear gendered school uniforms
	◆ Students are restricted from wearing clothes deemed "inappropriate" based on gender (e.g., a boy wearing a dress)
	◆ Students are prevented from wearing clothing supporting LGBTQ issues

(Cont.)

Table 7.2 Examples of Discriminatory School Policies and Practices Based on Gender (Cont.)

Extracurricular activities	◆ Gender-specific school athletics (e.g., different uniforms, different sports for boys and girls)
	◆ Gender-specific homecoming courts, prom kings/queens, and other types of gendered honors
	◆ Separation of boys and girls for music activities such as chorus, band, or orchestra with different dress requirements for performances
	◆ Students are prevented from attending a school dance with someone of the same gender
Exploring LGBTQ topics	◆ Students are prevented from discussing or writing about LGBTQ topics in class assignments or projects
	◆ Students are prevented from expressing LGBTQ issues in extracurricular activities such as the yearbook or school newspaper
Discipline	◆ The use of harsh and exclusionary discipline, such as zero tolerance policies
	◆ Students are disciplined for public affection that is not disciplined if it does not involve LGBTQ students
	◆ Students are unfairly disciplined at school for identifying as LGBTQ
Lack of support	◆ Victims' reports are ignored
	◆ Students are prevented from forming or promoting a Gay-Straight Alliance or official school club supportive of LGBTQ issues

said they'd also been bullied, harassed, or expelled because they were transgender or gender non-conforming at school" (n.p.).

Students who feel safe and supported at school have better academic and psychological outcomes. They report better school experiences, increased engagement, and more academic success. Gender-expansive youth need access to a curriculum inclusive of LGBTQ-related topics; sensitive and supportive educators; and schoolwide anti-bullying/harassment policies. Unfortunately, too many schools fail to provide these critical resources.

Many experts believe a curriculum inclusive of diverse groups, including gender identity and sexual orientation, instills a belief in the intrinsic worth of all individuals and in the value of a diverse society. Including LGBTQ-related issues in the curriculum in a positive manner sends a powerful message that LGBTQ students are valued members of the school community, resulting in a more positive and inclusive school climate (Human Rights Campaign, 2020). We must watch for gender stereotypes in books, films, and other media. It is very easy to find stories or novels which stereotype around gender issues—the cute little curly haired, blonde, blue eyed girl with the pink dress playing grownup as she sets the table, sweeps the floor, and rocks her baby doll. As she gets a little older she is seen studying to be a teacher, a nurse, or a secretary. While these are important careers, she could just as well be a doctor, engineer, or truck driver. Until recently, textbook publishers often illustrated their books with pictures that suggested stereotyped roles for young women and men. Passive, caring, and "following orders" types of roles were filled by females, while aggressive, physical, and "giving orders" types of roles were filled by males. Given the fact many children of color are from low-income families and may have less access to other books at home, the shortcomings of basal readers become even more significant.

It is imperative for classroom teachers to recognize their own biases regarding gender issues. Perhaps the girls in your classes sit quietly and raise their hands to answer questions, yet the boys shout out the answers. How do you make this inequality go away? If you do not recognize you are spending more than half of your classroom time working with either the boys or the girls, someone in your classroom is getting cheated. Several teachers were videotaped to help them become more aware of how they treat boys and girls differently. The results were surprising. First of all, the teachers used completely different terminology when speaking with boys, giving more extensive verbal feedback; and, when occasions arose, boys were given leadership roles, while the girls became followers. In one science classroom, an assignment was to complete several short experiments in groups of three or four students. One such group consisted of one young man and two young women. In each experiment, the young man did the actual microscope work and the two young women took notes and cleaned up the project when they were finished. It's time for a change!

Gendered school practices and discriminatory school policies reinforce the gender binary and gender stereotyping in school. These practices and policies perpetuate the idea that narrowly defined gender roles and heterosexuality are the norm and the only acceptable way of being. We argue teachers and school leaders have the power to disrupt this way of thinking. If we ensure our classrooms foster gender equity, acceptance, and inclusion, we can then help adolescents develop their identities in areas free from stereotypes and open to new ideas and challenges.

If a student reports an incident, don't ignore it. Be an advocate for that student. Work with all students to build community and create a positive school culture. School policies and practices that address in-school bullying, harassment, and assault are powerful tools for creating school environments where students feel safe. We must affirm and protect these students while providing an inclusive learning environment for all students. We must institute anti-bullying and anti-discrimination policies. We can support LGBTQ students by providing access to restrooms and locker rooms that recognize non-binary identities, and by welcoming students' preferred names and pronouns. Supporting our LGBTQ students and prioritizing their safety makes their success in school much more likely. We must make this happen.

Questions to Consider

1. How does our society socialize children to perform gender roles?
2. Does your school reinforce traditional gender role identification? If so, how?
3. How can we create a gender-inclusive classroom?
4. How do you feel about transgender students being required to use a particular bathroom?

Strategies for Teachers

♦ Middle-level teachers must be very watchful of the texts and trade books used in the classroom to ensure stereotyping by gender, role, race, or ethnic group is not present.

◆ Be aware of pronouns—are you constantly saying "he" when presenting math problems and "she" when working on writing?

◆ Check your textbooks—are there stereotypes regarding careers or lifestyles? Check your posters on the walls for non-traditional occupations, etc.

◆ Encourage non-traditional choices, i.e., girls taking shop classes or boys in home economics.

◆ Be sure you offer both cooperative and competitive activities to all students.

◆ Avoid traditional gender roles when assigning students chores.

◆ Have a co-worker observe your classroom and your teaching to see how much time you spend with either boys or girls. Do you call on boys or girls more often? Do you spend more time assisting boys or girls? Do you respond to boys and girls in the same way?

◆ Consider your own experience with gender. Are you uncomfortable around people who do not fit rigid definitions of "male" or "female?" Do you have any gender biases?

◆ Don't ask students to compete as "boys against the girls." This reinforces the boy/girl binary and forces students to choose sides.

◆ Ask your students to analyze ways in which gender norms are portrayed in books, television shows, movies, and magazines.

◆ Does your curriculum include neutral or positive representations of LGBTQ people?

◆ Investigate ways to create a gender-inclusive classroom. Do you communicate a non-binary understanding of gender to your students through the visuals in your classroom, the books you read, and the language you use?

◆ Gender-diverse kids face increased rates of harassment, bullying, assault, depression, drug abuse, self-harm, and suicide. How are you working to ensure the safety of your gender-diverse students? Find out if your school has a Gay-Straight Alliance (GSA).

References

Gay, Lesbian & Straight Education Network (2019). GLSEN releases school climate survey. Retrieved from http://www.glsen.org/article/glsen-releases-new-national-school-climate-survey.

Human Rights Campaign (2020). 2018 LGBTQ youth report. Retrieved from https://www.hrc.org/resources/2018-lgbtq-youth-report.

Kosciw, J. G., Greytak, E. A., Zongrone, A. D., Clark, C. M., & Truong, N. L. (2018). *School climate survey: The experiences of lesbian, gay, bisexual, transgender, and queer youth in our nation's schools.* New York, NY: GLSEN.

8

Intellectual Diversity

Case Study

Mr. Roberts was very excited about today's science lesson. He had planned the perfect PowerPoint lecture. It would cover all of the sixth-grade science standards related to electricity. He had carefully defined every vocabulary word with a quiz at the end. He had included illustrations of simple, series, and parallel circuits with all of the components labeled, just like the textbook. He had even found a cute graphic of a dog with an electric fan blowing his ears back. He was sure the students would love it. If he had time, he planned to demonstrate how to connect real wires to a battery, light bulb, fan, and switch. There was a brand new, unused class set of similar materials in the closet.

Mr. Roberts' first period class was very well behaved during the lecture, although two of the students fell asleep. His second and third period classes did not go so well. Several students were disruptive and had to be reprimanded. They just couldn't seem to sit still and listen. During his planning period, Mr. Roberts decided to rethink his lesson. His sixth period class was going to be a nightmare; all 32 students were below grade level; most were boys, and many were having discipline problems. He went to the closet and dusted off the box of materials. He dumped piles of wires, batteries, bulbs, motors, propellers, and switches on each table. When the students arrived, he simply said, "I challenge you to work in teams. If you can create circuits which work, I will explain how they work." Mr. Roberts was amazed to see how engaged his students were. One of his lowest-achieving students was actually the first to power up his fan. "If you need help," Mr. Roberts said, "go see Rashad. He's got it figured out." Rashad looked up, startled, and then gave his teacher a huge grin.

Chapter Content

Intellectual development refers to the ability to think, reason, and solve problems. During the middle-level years, students develop increasingly complex ways of thinking and first develop powers of abstract reasoning. They also become more skilled in metacognition, or thinking about thinking.

It is important for teachers to understand there are many different types of intelligence, and a single score on a standardized intelligence test is just one measure of a single facet of a child's intelligence. A single test score does not necessarily predict a student's ability to be successful in the future. In fact, it may not reflect the student's ability at all.

Dr. Carol Dweck (2006/2016) argues intelligence is not fixed or predetermined. Instead of being limited by one's innate "ability," our potential continues to grow as we try new things, experience challenges, receive constructive feedback, and are inspired by others' successes. From a growth mindset perspective, we can reframe, "I'm not good at fractions," to "I'm not good at fractions yet" (Mindset Works, 2017). Teachers who subscribe to "growth mindset" rather than "fixed ability" thinking can provide students with opportunities for rich experiences which can dramatically alter their achievement.

The human brain is a work in progress. Research shows how interaction with the environment actually changes the mass and organization of the brain (Jensen, 2005). Teachers who provide students with rich and diverse learning experiences are, in essence, brain changers and neural pathway connectors. This is especially important during the teen years, when the brain is undergoing rapid and dramatic development. Feinstein (2013) reminds us that adolescent brain development, not just hormones, helps explain teen behavior. Think about the following terms. Do you associate the following qualities with young adolescents?

◆ Problem-solving
◆ Judgment
◆ Inhibition
◆ Planning
◆ Emotional maturity
◆ Rational thinking
◆ Organization
◆ Attention
◆ Concentration
◆ Self-control

Skills such as planning, problem-solving, and organization are governed by the prefrontal cortex, which sits just behind the forehead and acts as the CEO of the brain. During adolescence, the pre-frontal cortex is still under construction. During this time, teens rely more heavily on the amygdala, which is part of the limbic system and is responsible for emotional reactions. The amygdala controls primal feelings such as fear and rage. Because they rely on the emotional area of the brain, adolescents tend to react in an impulsive manner rather than a reasoned one. The increased activity of the amygdala in teens may be because the frontal lobes have not yet developed a regulatory role in the nervous system. As the prefrontal cortex matures, teenagers become more skilled at reasoning, develop more control over impulses, and make better judgments. As this occurs, teachers should gradually reduce restrictions, non-judgmentally guide students toward reasonable choices, be prepared for some lapses as adolescents assume more responsibility, and help them learn from the consequences of choices which prove unwise.

Multiple Intelligences
Although experts do not agree on what constitutes intelligence, there is general agreement that different people learn differently. Howard Gardner (1999, 2011) suggests there are eight different

ways students learn. Individuals have all of these strengths, but in varying degrees. Despite some criticism and controversy around the multiple intelligences theory, we believe it is useful to broaden our understanding of intelligence using this framework. Thinking about different types of intelligence reminds us to vary our instructional strategies to teach diverse strengths. Gardner's categories include:

♦ Verbal-Linguistic: Special abilities in reading, writing, listening, and communicating with words (Word Smart)
♦ Logical-Mathematical: Reasoning, logic, problem-solving, numbers, patterns (Number Smart)
♦ Spatial: Visualizing, drawing, maps, imagining things (Art Smart)
♦ Bodily-Kinesthetic: Using body language and movement to express thoughts and ideas (Body Smart)
♦ Musical: Ability to perceive sounds, rhythm, tones, and musical patterns (Music Smart)
♦ Interpersonal: Ability to interact well with other people (People Smart)
♦ Intrapersonal: Understanding oneself (Self Smart)
♦ Naturalistic: Understanding and identifying nature (Nature Smart)

Robert Sternberg (1988) developed the triarchic theory of intelligence, which includes analytic, creative, and practical intelligence. Analytical intelligence refers to the ability to compare, contrast, analyze, and evaluate. Creative intelligence involves the ability to imagine, design, and invent. Practical intelligence is used to apply and implement ideas. Yet Sternberg notes that IQ tests only measure analytic intelligence. What about other types of intelligence, such as "street smarts" or emotional intelligence?

One way for middle-level teachers to help all students be successful is to design lessons and assessments which address multiple strengths, learning styles, modalities, and intelligences. They can strive to meet students where they are and get them where they need to be. Differentiated instruction may help the unique learning needs of students with special needs who may be gifted but have learning disabilities, making it difficult for them to work to their potential, or gifted students who often feel isolated.

What about the teacher who frequently uses cooperative learning techniques, but discovers a particular student prefers to work in isolation? Does the teacher insist the student work in a group because it more readily fits her teaching style, or does she allow the student to work individually as long as the student is learning and completing the work? Will the student be successful working in a group? Will the group be successful if all members do not participate? What about the highly intelligent student whose mother insists she would not work in cooperative learning groups with lower-achieving students? Does the teacher take the time to explain to the parent that all students, including the high-achieving kids, benefit from working in diverse groups?

Intellectual Disabilities

Students with intellectual, visual, or auditory disabilities present a type of diversity in the middle-level classroom that many teachers fail to acknowledge as diversity. When teachers state, "We have no diversity in our classroom; we are all alike," the question should be raised as to whether all students have the same intellectual, visual, and auditory capabilities. Is one student allowed to sit nearer the front to accommodate poor eyesight or poor hearing? Is tracking commonplace, thereby placing some students in classes which offer them more opportunities and others fewer opportunities? What about inclusion? If a school district upholds inclusion, thereby mainstreaming young people with learning disabilities, mental retardation, cerebral palsy, autism, and other exceptionalities into the regular classroom, there is indeed diversity in the classroom. These, too, are types of diversity which must be addressed if all students are to have equitable opportunities to learn and be successful.

How will you differentiate for varying rates of learning (e.g., early finishers), learning modalities (visual, auditory, kinesthetic, tactile), learning styles (e.g., verbal, logical-mathematical, spatial), and other relevant diversities (e.g., English language learners) in the classroom? What accommodations will you make to ensure access and academic success for students with disabilities such as autism, attention deficit disorder (ADD) or attention-deficit/hyperactivity disorder (ADHD), language impairment, intellectual disability, learning disability, visual impairment, or hearing difficulty? Accommodations are important tools for removing barriers (Table 8.1). Accommodations change *how* students learn, not *what* they learn. Modifications, on the other hand, change *what* the student is expected to know or learn. Only a student with an IEP or 504 plan would be required to have modifications. One way to remember the difference is this—accommodations level the playing field, while modifications change the playing field.

Table 8.1 Suggested Accommodations for Diverse Learners

Visual accommodations
◆ Encourage students with visual impairments to sit at the front of the classroom.
◆ Provide oral and written instructions.
◆ Provide access to instruction through tactile or auditory senses.
◆ Enlarge the text, sharpen contrast, and decrease visual clutter.
◆ Provide step-by-step directions with numbering and color coding.
◆ Allow a student to be tested orally and dictate her responses.

Auditory accommodations
◆ Encourage students with hearing difficulties to sit at the front of the classroom.
◆ Use a microphone so all students can hear.
◆ Use books on tape.
◆ Allow students to use a computer with talk-to-text capability.
◆ Provide audio recordings of lectures if needed.
◆ Use videos with closed-captioning.

Tactile accommodations
◆ Use maps, graphs, and diagrams with raised lines or dots.
◆ Use three-dimensional models.
◆ Provide hands-on experiences with real objects instead of pictures.
◆ Use a game which incorporates fine motor skills.
◆ Implement hands-on activities with manipulatives.

Kinesthetic accommodations
◆ Connect academic content to physical activity such as a simulation or role-playing.
◆ Offer choices including movement; for example, students may choose to describe, illustrate, or act out the functions of cell organelles or sequence events on a timeline.
◆ Use a game which incorporates gross motor skills and whole body movement.

Table 8.1 Suggested Accommodations for Diverse Learners (Cont.)

Other accommodations
♦ Allow students an alternative to writing such as an oral presentation or a comic strip.
♦ Break material down into smaller, more manageable parts.
♦ Provide a fill-in-the-blank outline of the lecture.
♦ Allow students to use highlighter markers to focus on key concepts.
♦ Provide graphic organizers and color-coded materials.
♦ Furnish an alternate text on a different reading level.
♦ Allow students to complete a shorter assignment.
♦ Reduce the number of choices on multiple choice tests.
♦ Allow students to receive extended time for tests.
♦ Grade assignments for content, not spelling, or provide a word bank.
♦ If possible, pair English language learners (ELLs) with a partner who is bilingual.
♦ Offer tightly structured lessons and alert students with autism or ADHD to prepare for transitions.
♦ Make sure you have students' attention before giving directions. Provide clear, concise directions orally and in writing. Ask students to repeat directions to check for understanding.
♦ Extend assignments for early finishers by offering opportunities for enrichment, not just more work.

More suggested accommodations are available at https://www.pacer.org/parent/504/.

Gifted and Talented

According to the federal Elementary and Secondary Education Act, gifted students are currently defined as "children or youth who give evidence of high-achievement capability in areas such as intellectual, creative, artistic, or leadership capacity, or in specific academic fields, and who need services and activities not ordinarily provided by the school in order to fully develop those capabilities" (National Association for Gifted Children, 2017, n.p.). The U.S. Department of Education estimates about 6% of public school students are receiving services for gifted and talented (GT) learners. These services may include "pull-out programs, advanced classes, varied grouping strategies, acceleration, differentiation of curriculum and instruction, dual enrollment, magnet schools, and specialized, self-contained schools (e.g., high schools for performing arts) (National Association for Gifted Children, 2017, n.p.).

There are a number of myths about gifted students, including the following:

♦ Gifted students don't need help; they'll do fine on their own.

◆ Gifted students make everyone in the class smarter by providing a role model.
◆ Gifted education programs are elitist.
◆ This student can't be gifted; he is receiving poor grades.
◆ Gifted students are always happy, popular, and well-adjusted in school.

The National Association for Gifted Children offers Pre-K-12 Gifted Education Programming Standards, which "increase the focus on diversity and collaboration—two powerful principles that guide high-quality programs and services. The standards use student outcomes for goals, rather than teacher practices, keeping them in line with the thinking in education standards generally. Because these standards are grounded in theory, research, and practice paradigms, they provide an important base for all efforts on behalf of gifted learners at all stages of development" (National Association for Gifted Children, 2017, n.p.). The Six Gifted Education Programming Standards include (1) Learning and Development; (2) Assessment; (3) Curriculum and Instruction; (4) Learning Environments; (5) Programming; and (6) Professional Development (National Association for Gifted Children, 2017).

Questions to Consider

1. What is intelligence?
2. What type(s) of intelligence are valued at school? Why?
3. What intellectual strengths do you have that might not be picked up by conventional measures of intelligence?
4. In what ways did your middle and high school classes take advantage of the advanced thinking abilities that develop in adolescence?
5. What do you believe about how students learn? Do you believe all students learn in the same way or at the same pace?
6. What do you believe about student ability? Does ability reflect the student's fixed potential to learn, or can it be changed?
7. What is it like to have a learning disability? Can a student have a disability in one area and be gifted in another?

8. Do you believe students should always be grouped by ability? Why or why not?
9. Do you believe teachers should adjust instruction to meet the needs of individual students, or should we be asking students to adjust to our teaching style?

Strategies for Teachers

♦ At the beginning of the year, take a class period to walk students through a "museum tour" of the textbook, pointing out its organization, photographs, and graphic features such as charts and tables.

♦ Teach students to use graphic organizers or color code text to categorize information and look for patterns. You might consider having students use two hula hoops to create a Venn diagram on the floor.

♦ Break down assignments into small segments; set short-term goals which lead to a larger objective.

♦ Teaching all students how to set goals should be a priority in every classroom. Starting out with small, reachable goals will allow for success and may help students set bigger and more enduring goals.

♦ Keep in mind that teens' brains crave predictability, novelty, relevancy, challenge, feedback, and opportunities for choice.

♦ Provide time for free choice reading. How many "down time" minutes a day could you reclaim for students to read? Even ten to fifteen minutes a day can really add up!

♦ Use cooperative learning groups which involve students from all learning abilities and styles. "Real life" is a community effort of people from all walks of life.

♦ Encourage students to see different perspectives by rewriting a story from multiple points of view.

♦ Use different groupings for different assignments. Consider switching up the criteria you use for assigning students to groups, such as artistic ability or public speaking skills.

♦ Remember individual differences. Is there an opportunity for less popular students to shine in the classroom? Is it possible to find strength in a student who is never a leader which would allow him or her to be a leader for a day?

◆ Plan to do an integrated or interdisciplinary unit with other teachers. If students can see how disciplines relate both to each other and to real life, learning will be more meaningful to them.

◆ Play a trivia or Jeopardy-style game to review academic content. Be sure the game is played for fun and not competitive.

◆ Consider allowing students to retake tests or revise and resubmit papers for partial credit to improve their grade.

◆ Give students opportunities to revise their work with meaningful feedback until they demonstrate mastery.

◆ To review material, ask students to design a few multiple-choice test questions.

◆ Ask students to summarize a lesson in a text message or a tweet.

References

Dweck, C. S. (2006/2016). *Mindset: The new psychology of success*. New York, NY: Penguin Random House.

Feinstein, S. G. (2013). *Secrets of the teenage brain: Research-based strategies for reaching and teaching today's adolescents* (2nd ed.). New York, NY: Skyhorse Publishing.

Gardner, H. (1999). *Intelligences reframed: Multiple intelligences for the 21st century*. New York, NY: Basic Books.

Gardner, H. (2011). *Frames of mind: The theory of multiple intelligences*. New York, NY: Basic Books.

Jensen, E. (2005). *Teaching with the brain in mind* (2nd ed.). Alexandria, VA: Association for Supervision and Curriculum Development.

Mindset Works (2017). Decades of scientific research that started a growth mindset revolution. Retrieved from https://www.mindsetworks.com/science/.

National Association for Gifted Children (2017). Retrieved from https://www.nagc.org/.

Sternberg, R. (1988). *The triarchic mind: A new theory of intelligence*. New York, NY: Viking Press.

9

Emotional Diversity

Case Study

Angie sat across the table from her English teacher, rapidly twisting strands of thin blonde hair around one finger. "Angie, look at me," said Ms. Cooke. "I don't understand why this happened. You were doing so well."

Still looking down, Angie whispered, "I had to protect myself." For the third time this year, three girls had attacked her in the bathroom. She had slipped a kitchen knife in her backpack that morning. She knew it might get her suspended again, but it was better than going home with another black eye. She couldn't help that Jason liked her better than Lisa. She hadn't led him on, although Lisa seemed to think so.

"Violence is never the answer," Ms. Cooke said.

"Where I come from, violence is the only answer," thought Angie, but she murmured, "Yes, ma'am."

The teacher reached for the girl's hand, but Angie tried to pull away. Her sleeve shifted to reveal a jagged network of ugly scars on her wrist. Some of them appeared to be fresh. Ms. Cooke's tone shifted. "How can I help you?" she asked softly.

"There's nothing you can do," Angie said. Then, she began to cry.

Chapter Content

Moodiness, restlessness, and erratic, inconsistent behavior are elements of middle-level students' emotional development. Even as they are supposedly rejecting their families and other adults, they are, in fact, seeking adult acceptance and searching for role models. At the same time, middle-level students tend to be idealistic and begin to ask questions about the meaning of life. Young adolescents often experience mood swings—not just on a daily basis, but almost minute by minute. The young adolescent's smile and good mood in homeroom may drastically change by lunchtime, or even by the end of the first period. Because young adolescents are immensely self-conscious, often lack self-esteem, and are so very sensitive, a single, negative remark or suggestion by a classmate can ruin an entire day. Why?

> From a biological perspective, as a result of changes in the adolescent brain, teens experience a significant increase in emotional intensity. At the same time, frontal lobe development lags behind changes in other brain areas so that they have difficulty modulating or 'damping down' the intense emotions they experience. Teens who have a history of weak emotional control are vulnerable to even more emotional turmoil than their peers.
> (Guare, Dawson, & Guare, 2013, p. 69)

Emotional well-being is tied directly to young adolescents' self-concept and self-esteem. If we perceive ourselves as a successful parent or teacher, our self-esteem is high. If, on the other hand, situations arise where we feel we are not successful in these self-appointed roles, our self-esteem could be nearer the bottom of the scale. If we apply this same definition to young adolescents in middle school, and if we consider the variety of roles to which they assign themselves every day, it is little wonder their self-concepts are not always at a high point. Every day young adolescents find it impossible to be the best student, the best athlete, the best daughter, and the wisest club leader, all at once. Given these impossible tasks, is it any wonder why young adolescents are on emotional roller coasters? Many feel if they fail to be the best in anything they do, then they have failed in everything they do. Middle-level students today, because of conditions not of their own making, find themselves dealing with stress not even considered by their age group a few years ago. For example, social media is a significant part of many adolescents' lives and can have a huge impact on their social and emotional well-being. They may obsess over the number of followers or "likes" they achieve on Snapchat, Instagram, or YouTube. This constant social media feedback can make them feel accepted, isolated, or bullied.

Self-Harm

Educators often face situations that fall well outside the scope of teaching and beyond the training they received. When depression and anxiety become overwhelming, some adolescents turn to self-harm. Self-harm, also known as self-injury, is one of the least understood risky adolescent behaviors and is growing at an alarming rate. Knowing how to support a student who self-injures can be a daunting responsibility for anyone.

An estimated 12–37% of adolescents engage in self-harming behavior. Initiation of the behavior is closely associated with puberty; people who self-harm usually start in early adolescence, between the ages of 11 and 15 (Retter, 2010). A recent large-scale meta-analysis of deliberate self-harm and non-suicidal self-injury cases from 1990 to 2015 found the mean age of starting self-harm was 13 years, with cutting being the most common type of injury (45%) (Gillies et al., 2018). The most frequent reason given was relief from negative thoughts or feelings. The vast majority of people who report non-suicidal self-injury do not try to end their life; they are trying to cope with life.

Self-injury is anything someone can do to purposely hurt their body. The most frequent sites of self-injury are the hands, wrists, stomach and thighs, though self-injurers may hurt themselves anywhere on the body. The most common types of self-injury include cutting, scratching, using cigarettes or matches to burn the body, carving words or symbols into the skin, hitting or punching oneself, head banging, rubbing an area excessively to create a burn, piercing the skin with sharp objects, pulling out hair, and picking at existing wounds (Crisis Text Line, 2020).

Experts say most adolescents engage in self-injury as a way to release painful emotions. And most self-injurers report it works—it calms them and brings a sense of relief. Why? Research suggests self-injury can activate different chemicals in the brain. In fact, the release of endorphins can produce feelings of euphoria for a brief period of time. Adolescents who self-harm report it distracts them from negative thoughts and feelings, helps them feel something physical when they feel numb, and gives them a sense of control over their lives (Gillies et al., 2018). Sadly, some report self-injury as punishing themselves for things they think they've done wrong.

The most obvious effects from self-injury arise from the wounds themselves, which pose a risk of uncontrolled bleeding, infection, and permanent scars. But, there are psychological consequences as well, including feeling guilt and shame about the behavior; experiencing a diminished sense of self; and believing they are helpless or worthless. Students may lie to others about the injuries and avoid friends and loved ones, further isolating themselves. Finally, self-injury can become addictive and spiral out of control.

What Should Teachers Do?

Know the signs. Students who self-harm are good at hiding it. Be alert for signs of the most common signs of self-injury or emotional distress including:

- ◆ Unexplained injuries, such as fresh cuts, scratches, bruises, or burn marks
- ◆ Wearing long sleeves or long pants to cover up all the time, even in hot weather
- ◆ Avoiding situations where they have to expose arms or legs, such as swimming
- ◆ Dramatic changes in mood, eating, or sleeping patterns

◆ Losing interest in friends and social activities
◆ Difficulties with interpersonal relationships
◆ Health complaints such as stomach pains and headaches
◆ Persistent questions about personal identity
◆ Behavioral and emotional instability, impulsiveness, or unpredictability
◆ Saying that they feel helpless, hopeless, or worthless
◆ Withdrawing from their usual life

Take action. Do not ignore anything suspicious. If your gut instinct tells you something is going on with a particular student, follow up on it.

Rely on the professionals. Notify the school counselor, social worker, and school administrators. Once a cutting habit has been formed, it is extremely difficult to break. Students may need professional help to learn other coping strategies.

Show you care. Be a consistent and supportive teacher and listen when they want to talk or vent. Let your student know you are there, but don't push too hard. Students who self-injure do not want to be cornered by adults.

Create a safe space for all. Create an environment that makes the students feel emotionally, physically, and psychologically safe every day. Offer support and help when students need it. Also, set clear boundaries about not tolerating name calling or any unkind behavior.

Teach coping strategies. Without calling attention to specific students, teach the class coping strategies. Help them identify ways to achieve release from stress such as mindfulness or physical exercise. Encourage students to write or draw about their feelings in a notebook.

Trauma-Informed Care

Poverty, violence, hunger, abuse, and an unstable world cause our students chronic stress and anxiety. According to a recent National Survey of Children's Health, nearly half the children in the United States—almost 35 million children—have experienced at least one or more types of serious childhood trauma (Resilient Educator, 2020). Some of our students have parents who are incarcerated, have mental health issues, or are addicted to drugs. Others are homeless, staying with relatives, or in foster care. Many of our students have witnessed or experienced situations we could never imagine. They are understandably traumatized. According to the Resilient Educator (2020), trauma can be categorized as follows:

1. Threat to life or limb
2. Severe physical harm or injury, including sexual assault
3. Receipt of intentional injury or harm
4. Exposure to the grotesque
5. Violent, sudden loss of a loved one
6. Witnessing or learning of violence to a loved one
7. Exposure to a noxious agent
8. Causing death or severe harm to another

Traumatic stress can severely impact a student's ability to learn, function in social environments, and manage their emotions and behaviors. Becoming a trauma-informed educator means becoming more acutely aware of how trauma alters the lens through which our students see and understand their world. Trauma affects children in different ways and can manifest in different behaviors. Some students become aggressive, while others suppress their pain. It is important to know our students' stories in order to help them. To support students who have experienced trauma, an emphasis must be placed on understanding, respecting, and appropriately responding to the effects of trauma. In short, relationships must be prioritized over content (Venet, 2018). As one teacher said, "If you're not addressing the trauma, and the students are distracted, checked out, and falling increasingly behind, even the best curriculum won't matter." Another teacher remarked, "When teachers fully understand trauma and its manifestations, the mindset will shift from one more thing to do to THE thing we must do."

The five guiding principles of trauma-informed care are safety, choice, collaboration, trustworthiness, and empowerment. The intention of trauma-informed care is not to address the specific traumatic event, but rather to provide support services in a way that is accessible and appropriate to those who have experienced trauma. Students need to feel they are safe, respected, and valued. Students who do not receive the care they need may actually be retraumatized, further compounding the problem.

Because they experience some of the most profound emotional changes in the lifespan, all young adolescents have an intense need to belong and fit in. As teachers, we must find ways to help our students feel securely connected, respected, and valued (Barron & Kinney, 2018). Students who feel a sense of belonging are more engaged, more resilient, and more successful. They have fewer behavior problems, fewer negative emotions in class, lower stress, and lower absenteeism (Barron & Kinney, 2018). To promote a sense of belonging, we must understand the nature of young adolescents, support our students' personal development, create a sense of community, and believe in our young people. We must respect their opinions and let their voices be heard while teaching them to respect the opinions of others. We must teach them leadership skills and give them opportunities to lead. Every student needs to feel loved, appreciated, and respected.

Questions to Consider

1. What do teachers need to know about their students? How can this information inform our teaching?
2. How can we give our students opportunities to regulate and control their own behavior?
3. How can we teach students to handle emotionally intense situations, conflict, criticism, and confrontation?
4. What are some examples of trauma our students may have experienced outside of their school?
5. How can we build positive, strong student-teacher relationships?

6. What should teachers do if they suspect a student is depressed, suicidal, or inflicting self-harm?
7. How can we teach our students strategies to cope with stress?
8. How might we give students alternatives and choices about what and how they learn?

Strategies for Teachers

◆ Greet each student at the door by name with a warm welcome.
◆ Play soft music as students enter the room.
◆ Start each class with a daily check-in. Ask, How are you feeling today? Hold up your fingers to show how you're doing on a scale of one to five. Or, select the emoji that best fits your mood today.
◆ Be clear and specific about your rules and keep the "have tos" to a relatively small number (Guare et al., 2013, p. 171).
◆ Use active listening and communication strategies which invite discussion rather than confrontation.
◆ Choose your battles. Negotiate or compromise when possible and explain your decisions. Avoid just saying no.
◆ Keep your cool. Don't get angry and escalate an emotionally intense situation.
◆ Be proactive and anticipate your students' feelings.
◆ Give students time and space to think and cool down.
◆ Share an emotional story from your own middle school days.
◆ Give students opportunities to write regularly in a journal to which you respond. This journal should be confidential so students will be encouraged to write freely.
◆ Ask students to take a stand on an emotionally charged issue, such as capital punishment, by lining up on an agree/disagree continuum. After they investigate the issue, ask them to line up again to see if their opinion has changed.

◆ Ask students to analyze the lyrics to a popular song, and connect it to a lesson.

◆ Ask students to explain why they don't like their parents' music and why their parents don't like theirs.

◆ Play an audio recording of Shel Silverstein's poetry. How does the author use language to make us laugh?

◆ Read children's literature aloud. How does the writer use language to convey feeling? How could you adapt this story to make a Disney movie?

◆ Teach conflict resolution.

◆ Help frustrated students set short-term, attainable goals.

◆ Role play how to channel emotions in positive ways.

◆ Group students into small learning communities with a mentor, advisor, or advocate to form close, trusting, and mutually respectful relationships.

◆ Start an advisory group—they want to know someone cares they are there and they can make a difference.

References

Barron, L., & Kinney, P. (2018). *Middle school: A place to belong and become.* Westerville, OH: Association for Middle Level Education.

Crisis Text Line (2020). How to deal with self harm. Retrieved from https://www.crisistextline.org/topics/self-harm/#what-is-self-harm-1.

Gillies, D., Christou, M., Dixon, A., Featherston, O., Rapti, I., Garcia-Anguita, A. … Christou, P. (2018). Prevalence and characteristics of self-harm in adolescents: Meta-analyses of community-based studies 1990–2015. *Journal of the American Academy of Child & Adolescent Psychiatry, 57*(10), 733–741.

Guare, R., Dawson, P., & Guare, C. (2013). *Smart but scattered teens: The "executive skills" program for helping teens reach their potential.* New York, NY: Guilford Press.

Resilient Educator (2020). Essential trauma-informed teaching strategies for managing stress in the classroom. Retrieved from https://resilienteducator.com/classroom-resources/trauma-informed-teaching-tips/.

Retter, R. (2010). Why do teens hurt themselves? The science of self-injury. Life Science, Future US Inc. Retrieved from https://www.livescience.com/11043-teens-hurt-science-injury.html.

Venet, A. S. (2018). The how and why of trauma-informed teaching. George Lucas Educational Foundation. Retrieved from https://www.edutopia.org/article/how-and-why-trauma-informed-teaching.

10

Social Diversity

Case Study

For the first time ever, Jimmy was excited for back to school shopping. He planned to discard all of his off-brand jeans and his dirty old sneakers, and he had his eye on a very cool, vintage David Bowie t-shirt which he felt perfectly expressed his personality. Plus, a new wardrobe would definitely give him the courage to talk to the popular kids instead of eating lunch alone as he had done every day last year.

But at the store, his mother disagreed. "Those jeans cost twice as much as your old pair and they have holes in them! David Bowie is a totally inappropriate role model for a child your age. There's no way you're wearing any of this to school." Instead, she picked out cheap jeans, plain sneakers, and t-shirts that looked exactly like the ones he had worn last year.

On the first day of school, Jimmy couldn't help but notice all of the new, vibrant clothes in the classroom. The rows of fresh white sneakers, stylish jeans (with holes in them!), and edgy t-shirts made his cheap, plain outfit feel like a humiliating costume he would be trapped inside all year long. It was impossible to focus on anything else.

When the lunch bell finally rang, Jimmy took one look at the popular kids' table before finding an empty spot in the corner of the cafeteria. He ate lunch alone.

Chapter Content

Identity and a sense of belonging are of utmost importance to 10- to 15-year-olds. If Jimmy has to go to school with jeans sporting the wrong label because that is all his family can afford, he is not only going to feel isolated but in all probability, will also endure a good amount of teasing by his peers. How will Jimmy sit in class and learn all there is to learn if he is concentrating on jeans, sneakers, or the new t-shirt he does not have? Are these students at risk? Are these the students who will "fall through the cracks" of our educational system? By the time students reach middle school, it is fair to say they know if they don't have the same opportunities as the rest of their peers. They know there is a good chance they won't ever finish high school. One young girl told her teacher she knew she wouldn't graduate anyway, so why not get pregnant now and be able to leave school? "At least I will have someone to love and someone who loves me." This must not be her only option.

Young adolescents constantly ask, "Who am I?" Who do you think I am? Where do I fit in this society? Where can I make a difference?" In response to the turbulent changes they experience in their physical and intellectual development, young adolescents experience dramatic changes in self-concept. More than anything else, young adolescents need to develop views of themselves as valuable, able, and responsible people. They use social comparison to compare themselves with others and measure their sense of self-worth. Van Hoose, Strahan, and L'Esperance (2009) point out,

> Young adolescents don't define themselves in a vacuum. Rather, they define their identity based, to a large extent, on how "significant" others convey their perceptions of them. Parents/caretakers, friends, teachers, and other family members play key roles in their personal development.... Identity acts as "an unfolding bridge" linking individual and society, childhood, and adulthood. (p. 45, 47)

Young adolescents want to be identified as individuals, yet conform to dress, attitude, and activities of their peer groups. The desire to interact comfortably with their peers, yet still be individuals with their own autonomy, is extremely critical in the lives of these young adolescents. Their loyalty shifts from family to peers; finding approval and encouragement from their peers is of utmost importance. Even when they feel adults do not believe or understand them, they still seek out adult role models, often using parental supervision as an excuse when they are unsure of situations in which they find themselves. For example, when asked to attend a certain party or go out with a group of peers, many times young adolescents will say, "My parents won't let me," secretly happy they don't have to do something they were really not sure they wanted to do, yet they have someone besides themselves to blame. They want to feel responsible for making their own decisions, but it is still important to be able to depend on parents for support.

Suddenly, they are dating and hanging out with their friends. It is sometimes difficult to figure out, however, just when they are going out, as dating is often restricted to school events, talking on the phone, or going to classes and lunch together. Of course, they can be "going out with" Jimmy or Joanne in the morning and all of a sudden, they are "going out with" Bill or Susan by afternoon. It is no laughing matter, believe me!

Middle-level students still depend on their families for their values. While they are firmly loyal to their peers, and in an attempt to be different, they actually become just like everyone else, which was the goal in the first place. As their friendships go through normal ups and downs, the adults in their lives must not interfere but help them to understand that one disagreement doesn't have to ruin a relationship.

In times of unhappiness when something has happened which affects any one of a group of young people, it is not uncommon to find all of them in a sad state of tears and distress. A teacher once asked a young girl why she was crying and her reply was, "Because Sandy is." If one is doing something, it is not uncommon for an entire group to be involved in doing the same thing, just because. No matter how many times young adolescents tell us they want to be different and "not like everyone else," when we observe a classroom or a cafeteria in a middle school, we wonder "where is the difference she was talking about?" They are all so different that they look exactly the same. The quickest way to be sure young adolescents wear the latest fad, however, is for any adult to tell them we don't like it. They will run to the nearest mall to buy whatever we said didn't look good—proof positive that if parents and teachers don't approve, their peers certainly will.

As young adolescents develop mental and physical maturity, many times their social skills are still in the beginning stages. The next time you see the young man with whom you previously discussed the philosophical reasoning behind Einstein's theory, he may be acting more like a three-year-old than a 13-year-old. You wonder, "Is this the same young man?" Yes, it is. It will take time for all of his attributes—physical, intellectual, emotional, and social—to catch up and develop before he becomes a mature young adult.

According to The Association for Middle Level Education (Bishop & Harrison, 2021), one of the most critical characteristics of young adolescents in their social development is their desire for recognition for their efforts and achievements. However, not all young adolescents want or will accept the same type of recognition. There is always something we can "catch a kid doing right" in order to acknowledge these young people, even if it is passing in homework for the first time that semester. Praising Johnny for his first good math paper or Sandy for her science project explaining the uses of electricity in space are equally as important. James, on the other hand, may not want any public acknowledgment at all. Young adolescents are extremely diverse in their accomplishments as well as in their need to be acknowledged. It is up to teachers to know their students and how they may best be helped. As stated earlier, young adolescents need to feel valuable if their existence is to have meaning. For Johnny and Sandy, sometimes even a pat on the back or a "well done" is all that is necessary to bring a smile to the face or a twinkle to the eye, whereas James may best be served by a simple nod of the head.

Early adolescence is also a time when 10- to 15-year-olds are searching for the values they will live by as they grow into adulthood. Because they are very emotional, very sensitive, and very aware of the world around them, young adolescents ask those complicated "why" questions of parents, clergy, coaches, and teachers. Answering a young adolescent's question with "because I said so" or "that's just the way it is" is not satisfactory. Because youth are in the process of moving from concrete to abstract thinking, they now have questions which may have no answers, or at least not black and white answers. With all the challenges they encounter, young adolescents deserve honest and straightforward answers from adults for questions they ask. Middle school students want to save the world. They are convinced they can find a way no one else has thought of to bring about change; and in some cases, they are successful. Environmental issues such as saving the rainforest and animal rights are perfect for middle-level students. They are extremely idealistic and passionately sure they can save the world, or at least make it a better place to be. Topics of this nature allow them opportunities to see connections between what they are learning and the world they live in—an important factor when choosing curriculum for middle-level students. We need to capitalize on their wide-ranging interests.

Finally, technology allows for virtual connections to be made with students from all over the world. Skyping, emailing, social media, and other forms of online communication can be effective tools to help students build broad social networks and encourage cultural exchange.

Questions to Consider

1. Were you taught to look an adult in the eye and say "Yes, ma'am" or "No, sir" as a sign of respect?
2. Do you become uncomfortable when someone stands too close to you?
3. Were you raised to value independence or did your background prepare you to work collaboratively for the good of the group?
4. What are the consequences of misinterpreting unfamiliar behaviors and punishing students without considering background differences?

5. Why is it important to provide opportunities for students to engage in social interaction?

Strategies for Teachers

◆ Use random-grouping strategies to assign different partners for brief, focused tasks daily. This will help them get to know one another and work with different people. You might use playing cards, paint color chips, puzzle pieces, "meet your match" vocabulary/definition cards, dominoes, or dice to have students find a partner.

◆ Have students analyze 15 minutes of a political debate, then identify key issues and stage their own debate. Consider randomly assigning students to defend a particular point of view after they prepare for both.

◆ Engage students in content area writing from different points of view using a Role, Audience, Format, Topic (RAFT) strategy. Working in small groups, the students select a role to play and as they think in that role, they have to communicate to a given audience using the format noted on the topic listed. This strategy requires students to process information and use critical thinking, rather than just write answers to questions.

◆ Plan virtual exchanges with other schools using Skype, WhatsApp, or Adobe Connect. Teachers from rural areas, inner city schools, or from around the world might arrange an exchange to learn more about their respective schools, communities, and cultures.

◆ Is social media causing problems in your school with Facebook, Twitter, Instagram? Cyber bullying? One school in Queens, NY, decided to hold a Delete Day as the seniors' end-of-year service project. They took over the school's computer lab and everyone was welcome during lunch or a free period to come in to get help cleaning up their online personas. There were no teachers looking over their shoulders so it was more comfortable for the students.

References

Bishop, P. & Harrison, L. (2021). *The successful middle school: This we believe.* Columbus, OH: Association for Middle Level Education.

Van Hoose, J., Strahan, D., & L'Esperance, M. (2009). *Promoting harmony: Young adolescent development and school practices* (3rd ed.). Westerville, OH: National Middle School Association.

11

Geographical Diversity

Case Study

Cindy grew up in New Jersey but moved to South Carolina in the eighth-grade. The culture shock was overwhelming. She had difficulty understanding her teachers' thick Southern accents, and the looks she got from her peers whenever she spoke made her feel like an outsider. "Where are you from?" they would ask. Cindy could almost hear them say, "And why are you here?" It was impossible to blend in.

One day Cindy asked her homeroom teacher if she could get a hall pass to go to the lav. "The what?" the teacher asked.

"The lav," Cindy replied.

"Why do you want to go to a lab?" Mr. Johnson asked. By now the rest of the students had stopped talking and were listening.

"I need to go to the lav," Cindy said quietly. Her face flushed red and she was keenly aware that all eyes were on her.

"I don't know what you mean," said Mr. Johnson.

"I need to go to the bathroom," Cindy whispered. She was mortified. In New Jersey, the "lav" was the lavatory. Never before had she had to say the word bathroom at school.

Chapter Content

A white 13-year-old moved from Maine to southwest Virginia. A white 12-year-old moved from the mountains of Tennessee to New York City. An African American student moved from Los

Angeles to southwest Colorado. A Chinese student entered a new school in South Carolina when his parents were hired at a local college. A 14-year-old Latino student entered a new school in Vermont mid-semester. Do these students add to the diversity in the classrooms they enter? Absolutely! Cultural differences, speaking accents, and dealing with connotations of words and phrases are different for students in new geographical areas and different cultural situations. To add to these scenarios, imagine the turmoil in the minds of young adolescents who do not speak English. The African American student moving to southwest Colorado might have to deal with issues of color as well as the meanings of words and phrases typically used in one area and not in another.

A regional dialect is a distinct form of a language spoken in a particular geographical area. Social dialects are associated with speakers belonging to a particular group. It is extremely important for young adolescents to belong to a social group. One way to do this is to emulate the word choices, pronunciation, and syntax of their peers. Acknowledging the importance of fitting in, middle-level students will go "to the ends of the earth" before letting a group of their peers know they don't know what is happening in the daily course of events. For example, young adolescents from Maine would ask for a soda. In Colorado, they would ask for a "pop." As minor as it might sound to an adult, to a middle-level student knowing the terminology is extremely important—another way to fit in.

Recently a student teacher prepared his first lesson plan on syllabication, and his teacher reminded him to remember his geographical location. Southwestern Virginians often use more syllables in their words than, for example, northern New Englanders who naturally shorten words in their vocabulary. A teacher from Maine who moved to Colorado and then to Virginia always begins her school year with, "If you don't understand something I say, be sure to ask me, because I will have to ask you, I'm sure." Adults are more apt to recognize they do not understand and then ask questions. Middle-level students are not as apt to speak up.

"Sit up straight and look at me when I'm talking to you!" How many times have you heard a teacher say this to a restless middle-level student whose main interest is anywhere except in that classroom at that particular time? What about the child whose culture discourages looking someone in the eye, especially one's elders? What about the child whose religion forbids looking at members of the opposite sex? All these factors must be taken into account when working with middle-level students. Likewise, this issue is critical when discussing, administering, and assessing standardized tests. Inner city middle schoolers, for example, have a much different background from a middle schooler from the Midwest or deep South. These conditions must be taken into consideration whenever we examine students' test results.

Questions to Consider

1. How might geographical background influence students' perspectives, communication style, and behavior?
2. What are some possible impacts of geographical differences on classroom interactions?

Strategies for Teachers

◆ Assign students to work in small groups. Ask them to brainstorm regional variations on words such as "pop," "subs," "shore," "buggy," "fixin," "wicked good," "y'all," etc. and then report out to the class.

◆ Ask students to create a teen slang dictionary, including texting acronyms, which could be shared with grandparents.

◆ Start an international students club. What questions might they have about local traditions and celebrations?

12

Religious Diversity

Case Study

Yasmin was already nervous enough about her first day of middle school, but now she was standing in the locker room as everyone else "dressed out" for PE class. In her traditional Muslim household, women are required to dress modestly, and she knew the school-issued shorts and t-shirt uniform she was currently holding in her hands definitely did not fit this requirement. However, she also knew that not dressing out would cost her a full letter grade in a class which should be an easy A.

As all the other girls cleared the locker room to warm up for class, Coach Davis noticed Yasmin sitting alone on the bench. She was still wearing her long-sleeved tunic, long pants, and a hijab.

"What's wrong?" asked Coach.

"I can't wear this," said Yasmin.

"It's the school's PE uniform," said Coach. "It's required."

"My religion requires me to wear a hijab and clothes that cover my body," said Yasmin. She took a deep breath. "And my religion is more important to me than my PE grade."

The coach thought for a moment. "Would you prefer to wear the school's winter uniform today?" she asked gently. "We do have long sweatpants and a long-sleeved shirt."

"Yes please!" Yasmin exclaimed. Then, after a pause, "Can I still wear my hijab?"

"Of course," Coach Davis said. Yasmin happily changed into her uniform and rushed to join her classmates in the gym.

Chapter Content

With increasing numbers of young adolescents from diverse cultures, religions, and ethnicities attending classes together, it is important the majority culture not set expectations and standards to which all middle-level students cannot comply. Often middle school students' emotional well-being hinges on being accepted in such areas as dress, food, and holiday. If students have different religious or ethnic beliefs concerning fashion, how boys and girls interact with each other, or with certain holidays, it is important these differences are recognized and those who believe in them are not made to feel less important or embarrassed. If school lunches are served without consideration of certain religious holidays and beliefs, it is equally important to be sure alternative choices are available. Some choices we make inadvertently cause students to have low self-esteem, or feel left out. When students are asked, "What are some of the traditions you observe at Christmas?" are we asking only the Christians in the class to answer? What about the Jewish students, the Muslim or Seventh Day Adventist students? All students need to be included when planning celebrations of any nature.

At the beginning of the school year, Betty had all her students in the advisory program tell her their birthdays. Each one then had the option of what type of dessert he or she would like to share with the group—ice cream, cake, pie, cookies, Baked Alaska, fudge, or whatever else they might choose. On the appointed day, she would bring in the birthday dessert, and the whole group would celebrate. However, one year Betty was brought up short—one of her new students belonged to a religion which did not celebrate birthdays, Christmas, or any other holiday. As a rural Mainer, this was her first experience with this religious belief. It certainly made her stop and think about how this young man could be included and still not compromise his family's religious beliefs. How could she sustain his emotional well-being and still have him accepted by his peers?

Halloween is another celebration which causes some groups to question activities which occur in our schools. It is extremely important to be very careful not to offend those families who are concerned about witchcraft and Satanism. As innocent as the customs of Halloween may seem, the idea of going door-to-door asking for handouts may be very insulting and offensive to some people. Many schools have now disallowed Halloween celebrations in schools, turning instead to UNICEF collections, community family events, and in some cases, no celebrations at all. As the Easter season arrives, what a wonderful opportunity to also discuss Passover and perhaps invite persons of various faiths to talk to the class. How much more acceptance and recognition would students feel in this instance? Do we have children of other faiths who have similar holidays? Do some research and celebrate that day or season as well.

The number of Christians in the U.S. population is declining, while the number of U.S. adults who do not identify with any organized religion is growing, according to The Religious Landscape Studies (Pew Research Center, 2015). A recent extensive survey found the percentage of adults ages 18 and older, who describe themselves as Christians, has dropped by nearly eight percentage points, from 78.4% in 2007 to 70.6% in 2014. Additionally, the percentage of Americans who identify as religiously unaffiliated—describing themselves as atheist, agnostic or "nothing in particular"—has jumped more than six points, from 16.1% to 22.8% (Pew Research Center, 2015). Younger generations claim less religious affiliation than older generations. The survey found 34–36% of Millennials between the ages of 18 and 33 are religiously unaffiliated.

Judaism

Is Judaism an organized set of beliefs, a religion, a culture, or an ethnicity? Actually, it is all of these (Rich, 2016). A Jew is any person whose mother was a Jew or any person who has gone through the formal process of conversion to Judaism. Common ancestry is not required.

A Jewish rabbi is a religious teacher and scholar who is authorized to instruct the community and make decisions on issues of *halakhah* (Jewish law).

Kashrut is a Jewish law dealing with what foods Jews can and cannot eat, and how those foods must be prepared. Certain animals may not be eaten at all such as pigs, rabbits, shellfish, birds of prey, and insects (Rich, 2016). The animals which may be eaten must be slaughtered humanely, and all blood must be drained or broiled out before it can be eaten. Meat cannot be eaten with dairy; pots, pans, utensils, potholders, sinks, towels, and dishwashers which come in contact with meat must be kept separate from dairy products. Fruits and vegetables must be inspected for insects. Products certified as kosher are labeled with a mark called a *hekhsher*, which identifies the rabbi or organization that certified the product. Kosher dietary laws are observed all year round. According to a National Jewish Population Survey (NJPS), "21% of American Jews report they keep kosher in the home. This includes the vast majority of people who identify themselves as Orthodox, as well as many Conservative Jews and some Reform Jews" (Rich, 2016, n.p.)

A Jewish boy comes of age and is responsible for observing the commandments when he becomes a bar mitzvah at the age of 13 years. A Jewish girl comes of age and reaches her bat mitzvah at the age of 12. "Bat" means daughter in Hebrew and Aramaic and is pronounced "bas" (Rich, 2016). Bar Mitzvah literally means "son of the commandment." However, the term is now more commonly used to refer to the coming of age ceremony itself.

It is an ancient practice for Jews to cover their heads during prayer. The Yiddish word yarmulke means "skullcap." In Eastern cultures, it is a sign of respect to cover the head. Wearing a yarmulke in the synagogue is a custom, not a requirement.

Major Jewish holidays include Rosh Hashanah, Yom Kippur, and Chanukkah. Rosh Hashanah is the Jewish New Year. The holiday starts at sunset, the night before the day shown on the secular calendar. It is offensive to schedule important events, meetings, or tests on Rosh Hashanah.

Yom Kippur is the Jewish Day of Atonement. It occurs on the ninth day after the first day of Rosh Hashanah. It is a day of fasting and repentance. This holiday starts the evening before the day it appears on the secular calendar. Like Rosh Hashanah, most American Jews expect teachers to be aware of this day, and almost all will be offended if you schedule important activities on this day or the evening before (Rich, 2016).

Chanukkah is the Festival of Lights, commemorating the rededication of the Temple in Jerusalem after a successful revolt against the Greeks. As part of the rededication, the victorious Jews needed to light the Temple's menorah (candelabrum), but they had only enough oil to last one day and it would take eight days to prepare more oil. Miraculously, the one-day supply of oil lasted for eight days. The miracle of the oil is commemorated with this eight-day candle lighting holiday. Chanukkah begins between Thanksgiving and Christmas. Although almost nobody takes off from work or school for this holiday, many may not want to work nights or travel during the holiday so they can light candles with the family, and accommodations should be made for this (Rich, 2016). Traditions include lighting a nine-branched ceremonial lamp; playing games with a dreidel (a small four-sided spinning top with a Hebrew letter on each side—*nun, gimmel, hey,* and *shin*); winning chocolate coins (*gelt*); and eating potato pancakes (*latkes*). The most important thing to remember about Chanukkah is that it is not Jewish Christmas, no matter what the card shops and toy stores want you to believe (Rich, 2016).

Islam

Islam is an Arabic word, which means peace through submission to God. The Arabic word for God is Allah. Islam is "a religion of justice, peace, mercy, and forgiveness, a faith which is often misunderstood and misrepresented" (Seda, 2017, n.p.). Followers of Islam are called Muslims. The Qur'an is the holy book and sacred scripture of Islam. For Muslims, Islam is not just a religion, but a way of life.

A Muslim is required to pray five times a day—at dawn, mid-day, mid-afternoon, at sunset, and after nightfall. When

Muslims pray, they must always face Mecca (Makkah). Schools can accommodate this requirement by providing time and a private space for prayer.

Muslims observe two major religious holidays during the year. One of them is Ramadan. During the month of Ramadan, Muslims must fast from dawn to sunset. Schools can support these students by allowing them to go to the library or study hall instead of the cafeteria during lunch (Ali, 2007). Additionally, the religious dietary laws of Islam require Muslims to eat *Halal* (kosher) meat, which has been slaughtered according to Islamic requirements (Ali, 2007). Accordingly, schools should offer other choices when serving pork and pork products.

Islam prescribes a modest dress code. A Muslim woman must cover her hair and wear loose, unrevealing clothing. In Western society, the head covering is seen as a sign of oppression, which is an inaccurate assumption. A woman who dresses this way "commands respect, and through her modesty rejects sexual servitude. The message the woman gives when she wears Islamic dress in society is "Respect me for who I am. I am not a sex object" (Seda, 2017, n.p.). However, the Islamic dress code can be a source of tension at school. Many female Muslim students will wear a scarf as a symbol of religious identification and modesty. The Islamic tradition forbids indecent exposure and mingling between members of the opposite sex. Imagine how uncomfortable a Muslim student would feel in a co-ed physical education class, which requires students to wear shorts and short sleeve T-shirts.

Questions to Consider

1. As a child, did you attend a church where you were expected to sit quietly and listen, or was active participation and physical movement the norm?
2. What assumptions do we make about religious practices which are different than our own?
3. How might we recognize and respect religious beliefs and traditions from a pluralistic perspective?

Strategies for Teachers

♦ Investigate religious differences in your community. Have your students conduct a demographic survey to discover how many different religious groups there are. Then, do research on the individual groups to become aware of their histories.

♦ Invite local religious leaders to your classroom to discuss traditions, customs, and beliefs of their religions.

♦ Keep in mind that during the Christmas holidays, non-Christian students may feel isolated when participating in mainstream Christmas celebrations.

♦ Educators should be aware of Jewish dietary restrictions and should not schedule events on Jewish holidays (including the evening before).

♦ Educators should be familiar with the basic teachings of Islam and its practices. They should be aware of the dress code and dietary restrictions of Muslim students.

♦ Refrain from using the term "Islamic terrorist." Every religion has fundamentalist factions.

♦ Help your students realize we are a nation of immigrants; diversity is a great strength.

♦ We need to teach our students to think critically and challenge the fears, assumptions, and anger about religious intolerance and violence in our world.

References

Ali, P. J. (2007). Muslims in American schools: A guide for teachers. *Pennsylvania Teacher Educator, 6*, 10–16.

Pew Research Center (2015). America's changing religious landscape. Retrieved from http://www.pewforum.org/2015/05/12/americas-changing-religious-landscape/.

Rich, T. R. (2016). Judaism 101. Retrieved from http://www.jewfaq.org/index.shtml.

Seda, P. (2017). Islamic Center of Columbia: Masjid al-Muslimiin. What is Islam? Retrieved from http://www.almasjid.com/content/islamic_dress_code.

13

Developing a Diverse Curriculum

Case Study

Mrs. Jones posted two large signs on opposite sides of her seventh-grade classroom. One sign said "Agree" and the other sign said "Disagree." Mrs. Jones explained there were no right or wrong answers and read the following statements aloud. Each student was asked to take a stand along the Agree/Disagree continuum for each statement.

1. Public schools should require all students to wear uniforms.
2. Video games make teens violent.
3. Most adults do not respect teenagers.
4. The media unfairly portrays certain groups of people.
5. Prejudiced people cannot be changed.
6. Anyone who wants to come to the United States should be allowed to enter.

After the continuum activity, Mrs. Jones divided the students into small groups and asked them to record answers to the following questions:

1. How did it feel to take a position on some of the topics?
2. If there was a particular topic you were unsure about, what information would you need in order to form an opinion?

3. How did you feel when you saw others taking a completely different position from yours on a topic?
4. Do you think people sometimes pretend to agree with another person in order to avoid conflict?

Finally, Mrs. Jones led a class discussion, asking the students to consider ways in which people come to hold their beliefs, opinions, and values. She compiled a list of their responses on the board and asked them each to write a reflection.

Chapter Content

Curriculum is the most important component of any school; working in conjunction with organizational and school climate, the curriculum stands the biggest chance of making profound changes in student learning. Curriculum which meets the needs of young adolescents is based on criteria of high quality which provides direction for what young adolescents should know and be able to do and helps them achieve the attitudes and behaviors needed for a full, productive, and satisfying life (Bishop & Harrison, 2021). Banks and Banks (2016), in the excellent curriculum resource on culturally competent teaching in "transformative" and "social action" approaches to changes in classroom curriculum, suggest four levels for integrating ethnic content into the curriculum.

Level 1: Contributions Approach. This approach is characterized by adding ethnic heroes into the curriculum, but limited primarily to special days, weeks, and months related to ethnic events and celebrations. Students study little or nothing about the event or celebration before or after the occasion, and the curriculum remains unchanged in terms of its basic structure, goals, and characteristics. These events and issues are considered "add-ons" to the core curriculum. The contributions approach also tends to miss important concepts and issues related to cultural groups, and often results in reinforcing stereotypes and misconceptions by stressing the strange and exotic. Banks and Banks (2016) note,

"The criteria used to select ethnic heroes for study and to judge them for success are derived from the mainstream society and not from the ethnic community" (p.142). Activities of this type often include surface attention given to well-known cultural heroes and heroines such as Sacajawea, Booker T. Washington, Cesar Chavez, or Benjamin Bannaker. Teachers might feature a unit on "Native American Heroes," or "Women Who Have Made a Difference." Cultural foods, dances, and music are added to the curriculum.

Level 2: Ethnic Additive Approach. Without changing the basic structure, purposes, and characteristics of the curriculum, cultural events and issues are added using the perspective of mainstream culture. These additions do not include views and perspectives from diverse cultural groups, nor illustrate the roles played by these groups in the history and formation of society as we know it today. Banks and Banks (2016) call this the "illusion of inclusion." Activities at level 2 include strategies from the contributions approach mentioned earlier, adding a book or video to the curriculum with no change in perspective, including words and phrases from other cultures such as spelling lists, and having a class cooking project using recipes from different cultures (Banks & Banks, 2016). While levels 1 and 2 are relatively simple add-ons to the curriculum, some would argue any step taken to include ethnic and multicultural materials and information is better than ignoring it completely.

Level 3: Transformative Approach. This approach differs primarily from levels 1 and 2 because the curriculum is changed to allow students to study concepts, issues, themes, and problems from different perspectives, thus extending their understanding of the roles played by various ethnic and cultural groups in American society. Activities for level 3 include studying the perspective of all stakeholders in national and local events, or contrasting the reasons for the patterns of migration to the United States for people of Italian, Asian, Slavic, and African descent.

Level 4: Social Action Approach. This approach uses all the components of the Transformative Approach but adds more student decision-making and social action-related activities regarding the concept or issue being studied. This approach requires a great deal of change in the curriculum to include materials and resources to precipitate desired outcomes— social responsibility and justice—from students.

The levels and activities suggested in each approach are excellent beginning points for creating a positive and accepting classroom climate and for extending the curriculum. A word of caution— while they may seem beneficial, these activities can reinforce the notion that ethnic studies are not important enough to be part of the everyday curriculum. But it is the teacher's responsibility to push the level of integration ahead. Some classes are stuck at level 1, focusing only on heroes like Martin Luther King, Jr. for Black History Month, or holidays such as Cinco de Mayo. When a teacher attempted to educate her students about African American history other than during February, a student asked, "Why do we have to learn about black history, when we don't learn about white history?" It's definitely time for a change! One way to move from level 1 to level 4 is to ask students how they want to integrate content and on which issues they want to take action. Middle-level students become intensely involved when they work on issues from real life—issues which involve them and their futures. But remember, change is a process. It will take time and much work to move from level 1 to level 4. The important point is to realize and determine it is time to begin the change—now!

Professional associations such as the Association for Middle Level Education (AMLE) publish newsletters with online resources to assist teachers in designing a more diverse curriculum. A Maine school district developed a program called Open Waters, Safe Harbors, in which students interviewed senior citizens in the community and made a video of the interviews for teachers to use in their classrooms. One particular interviewee, a German Jew, had escaped to the U.S. during the Holocaust. This gentleman agreed to speak to several middle school classes as part of the Holocaust Unit. Did this make more of an impact than simply reading from a textbook? Of course, it did!

Students need opportunities to learn about other cultures, religions, races, and philosophies. They not only need to learn how it feels to be different, but they also need to learn it is all right to be different. As a consequence, teachers from middle-level schools are spending more and more time in professional development activities, attending meetings and workshops to find ways to help their students learn to work and cooperate with persons who are different from themselves. Universities and colleges are providing a new commitment to diversity in preparing teachers. They are also reaching out to diverse populations in order to present a more accurate representation of school districts with large multicultural populations.

Students in a Colorado middle school, for example, spent time in their school library analyzing fiction about stereotypes by studying book covers and predicting how issues of race and gender would be presented and what topics the books would cover. Another class had a "word for the day" noting anniversaries of special accomplishment, such as the first woman senator. As the culminating activity of an advisory project at a Maine middle school, students and teachers created a school-wide multicultural fair offering samples of foods, music, fashions, occupations, and much more from countries around the world. In helping students learn how to live and work with people from different cultures, one middle school established student peer mediation groups to aid other students who had problems dealing with differences. The predicament facing educators today, however, is we are still not doing enough to provide a safe, caring, trusting learning environment for our students, teachers, staff, and parents. What next? How and where do we go from here?

An excellent resource for educators is Teaching Tolerance (2020). Teaching Tolerance offers professional development, a magazine, and free classroom materials, including lessons, leveled student texts, films, and printable posters on topics such as race and ethnicity, religion, class, immigration, gender, and sexual identity. Their approach emphasizes anti-bias, equity, and social justice. Their mission is to eradicate intolerance and help teachers "create civil and inclusive school communities where children are respected, valued and welcome participants" (n.p.). They define tolerance this way:

> Tolerance is respect, acceptance and appreciation of the rich diversity of our world's cultures, our forms of expression and ways of being human. Tolerance is harmony in difference.

Questions to Consider

Banks and Banks (2016) suggest the following guidelines to check curriculum for bias:

1. Does the curriculum include content which will encourage students' self-awareness, regardless of sex, race, culture or disability?
2. Are the perspectives and contributions of diverse racial and cultural groups, both men and women, as well as those with disabilities, included?
3. Does the curriculum include activities or units dealing with the recognition of stereotyping and prejudice when they appear in written and oral language?
4. Are there activities which assist students in analyzing the mass media for ethnocentrism, sexism, or stereotyping of those with disabilities?
5. Do speech and composition activities include content which helps students speak and write in a non-sexist and culturally sensitive manner?
6. Is there career-oriented content that encourages the exploration of a broad range of careers, regardless of students' sex, race, culture, or disability?

Strategies for Teachers

◆ Plan a multidisciplinary unit on your hometown. Math activities could include collecting demographics on something as simple as the number of telephones, televisions, or pets. For science activities, students could test the drinking water. In social studies, students might investigate the history of the town and where the original inhabitants came from; in language arts, students could create an original play using all these facts from the different disciplines. Include technology, industrial arts, and home economics or life skills content as well as music and physical education activities to enhance the unit.

◆ Plan thematic units using questions such as these:
  • Is there prejudice in your town, school, or classroom? How can you and your students change it?
  • How diverse is your town, school, or classroom? How can you celebrate its diversity?

◆ Contact friends or relatives in another state who might speak to a local teacher. Investigate e-mail sites where a teacher could help students select pen pals from other states or countries.

◆ Produce a play which compares the Civil Rights era of the 1960s with current civil rights legislation.

◆ Use classroom-friendly documentaries and podcasts to explore diversity and social justice, available at www .tolerance.org/.

◆ Using newspaper accounts of recent hate crimes, set up a courtroom scene whereby there is a jury, judge, accuser, and accused, as well as a reporter. Following courtroom procedure, try the case and report the results.

◆ Invite speakers from cultural groups in your community to speak to your classes. Ask parents representing various ethnic groups to speak to the class about traditions, foods, and beliefs.

◆ Rewrite a scene from Romeo and Juliet and set the story in your hometown in modern times.

References

Banks, J., & Banks, C. (Eds.). (2016). *Multicultural education: Issues and perspectives*, (9th ed.). Boston, MA: Allyn & Bacon.

Bishop, P., & Harrison, L. (2021). *The successful middle school: This we believe*. Columbus, OH: Association for Middle Level Education.

Teaching Tolerance (2020). Retrieved from https://www.tolerance.org/.

14

Differentiating Instruction

Case Study

When Ms. Kelly's class returned from Christmas break, they learned a sixth-grade student at their school had been involved in a terrible car accident. He had sustained a spinal injury and would be in a wheelchair for the rest of his life. Because Westside Middle School was an old building and not handicap accessible, the school district planned to transfer him to a different school across town.

Ms. Kelly tried to get her social studies lesson started, but quickly realized her students needed the opportunity to talk about what had happened.

"Ms. Kelly," said Shawn. "It's not fair! Joseph has to leave his friends and go to a different school where he doesn't know anyone." Another student chimed in, "He's already been through enough!" Ms. Kelly responded, "Unfortunately, this old building has stairs to every single entrance."

Jacob said, "We should get the school to build him a ramp!" But another student shut him down. "A ramp costs way too much money. They'll never do it for just one kid." Ms. Kelly asked, "Well, what do you think *we* could do about it?"

After brainstorming for several minutes, the class decided to divide into teams. Each team would tackle one piece of the puzzle. One group of students offered to write letters to the principal, the school board, and their representative in Congress. A group of students who were on the math team offered to go outside to measure the entrance, calculate the slope, and design a proposed wheelchair ramp. Another team decided to research the Americans with Disabilities Act (ADA) compliance and safety standards. The fourth team offered to help build the ramp. The fifth group planned to organize a car wash and a bake sale to raise money for building supplies.

As the class period came to an end, Ms. Kelly realized this experience probably couldn't have happened in a second-grade classroom. She recognized though these middle school students were incredibly diverse, they had all come together to bring their different strengths and talents to solve a real-world problem. She realized these young adolescents were smart, creative, and compassionate. Ms. Kelly thought maybe she was meant to teach middle school after all.

Chapter Content

Consider the following questions: What is fair? Does being fair mean giving every student exactly the same curriculum and exactly the same instruction? Or does being fair mean giving every student exactly what they need to achieve their highest potential?

Every student brings something different to the table.

Differentiation is not just a teaching strategy. Differentiation is a way of thinking about teaching and learning (Tomlinson, 2014). It means responding to the needs of all learners and "adjusting lessons for students who struggle, learn differently, or need more challenge" (Wormelli, 2007, p. 4). It entails recognizing and removing barriers to learning, tailoring instruction for individual needs and interests, identifying potential, using flexible groupings, and building on student success. In short, differentiation means "doing whatever it takes to maximize students' learning instead of relying on a one-size-fits-all, whole-class method of instruction" (Wormelli, 2007, p. 9).

Teachers in differentiated classrooms use a variety of pedagogical (instructional) strategies and provide specific alternatives for individual students. They are "diagnosticians, prescribing the best possible instruction based on both their content knowledge and their emerging understanding of students' progress in mastering critical content. These teachers are also artists who recognize that students are individuals and require a personal fit" (Tomlinson, 2014, p. 4). Teachers can differentiate through content, process, and product. They do so by assessing each student's readiness, interests, and learning profile or preferred approaches to learning (Tomlinson, 2014). It is important to note that readiness is not fixed ability. Readiness can be changed by offering students' meaningful experiences and opportunities for growth. Differentiated instructional strategies include scaffolded assignments, tiered assignments, a menu of options, learning contracts, small-group instruction, and independent projects. For a list of suggested instructional strategies, see Table 14.1.

A powerful way to meet the unique developmental needs of young adolescents is by offering opportunities for kinesthetic learning. Kinesthetic strategies offer purposeful learning experiences as an alternative to whole-class lecture. Physical movement and social interaction are essential in the middle school classroom. Kinesthetic learning is an instructional strategy which connects physical movement and social interaction to specific academic content. The goal is to get students actively engaged and "learning by doing" as they investigate concepts by moving their bodies. After all, we want our students "to be intellectually active rather than mindlessly and passively receiving information" (Edwards, 2016, p. 26).

Table 14.1 Suggested Pedagogical Strategies for Differentiation

◆ Anticipation guide	◆ Direct instruction/lecture	◆ Mnemonic device
◆ Brainstorming	◆ Demonstration	◆ Drawing/artwork
◆ Graphic organizer or concept map	◆ Hands-on activity/manipulatives	◆ Movement
◆ Structured note-taking	◆ Small groups	◆ Music
◆ Analyze image, photo, or object	◆ Inquiry stations	◆ Multimedia—video, audio
◆ Annotate or highlight text	◆ Gallery walk	◆ Role-play
◆ Guided practice	◆ Turn and talk	◆ Game
◆ Quick writes	◆ Think-pair-share	◆ Project

Wormelli (2007) outlines specific steps to take before, during, and after designing the learning experience. The "before" steps include identifying essential understandings, questions, and/or standards; identifying students who have special needs; and designing formative and summative assessments. The "during" steps include analyzing the students' pre-assessment data; planning a logical sequence; conducting the lesson; and making adjustments as needed, based on observations and formative assessment data collected while teaching the lesson. The "after" steps include working with students to evaluate the lesson, asking questions—What worked? What didn't work? Why? What changes would you make next time?

Pre-assessment is used to determine student readiness, prior knowledge, and interests. Also called diagnostic assessment, pre-assessment helps us understand where our students are, and where they need to be. This is crucial for making decisions on how to differentiate content, process, and product. Pre-assessment is used to guide instruction but can also be used as a warm-up to get students engaged and interested in learning more about the topic.

Formative assessment helps us determine what our students have mastered, what they still need, and what needs to happen next. Assessment is formative "when the evidence gathered is used to adapt instruction to meet student needs" (Blaz, 2013, p. 23). Formative assessment should be differentiated to meet the needs of your students. For example, teachers who have a classroom full of kinesthetic learners may wish to modify their formative assessments to incorporate movement such as dramatizing a concept. Auditory learners will likely benefit from oral questioning. Visual learners may respond well to color coding or highlighting text.

Summative assessment is used to evaluate individual student growth and development and generally receives a grade. Traditionally, this means administering a quiz or a test. When testing, be sure to offer different types of tests such as multiple choice, matching, fill-in-the-blank, and short answer/essay, as opposed to having the same format on every test. In addition, you might consider giving students the option to draw or illustrate a concept as opposed to writing a description. Another type of summative assessment is "performance-based assessment, in which students display knowledge by using concepts and skills in an authentic context" (Blaz, 2013, p. 55). This might include projects and portfolios which are assessed using pre-stated criteria on a rubric or checklist. Ultimately, teachers should aim to give students multiple opportunities to be assessed using methods of their own choice, so they can demonstrate their competencies to the best of their ability. For a list of suggested assessment strategies, including diagnostic, formative, and summative assessment options, see Table 14.2.

Benjamin (2002) offers the following characteristics or "teacher habits of mind" needed to differentiate instruction (pp. 11–13):

1. As a teacher, I revise and reflect.
2. I encourage lots of student talk.
3. I offer choices and alternatives.
4. I believe in reading and model the joy of reading.
5. I say, "This reminds me of…" to make connections to prior knowledge.
6. I am interested and curious about learning in general.
7. I value diversity and offer an inclusive curriculum.

Table 14.2 Suggested Assessment Strategies for Differentiation

Diagnostic Pre-assessments	Formative Assessments	Summative Assessments
◆ Whole group warm-up review	◆ Ask open-ended questions	◆ Student sheet
◆ Student interest survey	◆ Listen in small groups	◆ Quiz
◆ KWL chart	◆ Hold student conferences	◆ Test
◆ Think-pair-share	◆ Hand signals/thumbs up	◆ Project
◆ Quick writes	◆ A/B/C/D flip card	◆ Portfolio
◆ Pre-test	◆ Students hold up a whiteboard	◆ Scoring sheet
◆ Checklist	◆ Peer editing	◆ Rubric
◆ Review game	◆ Self-evaluation	
◆ Graphic organizer	◆ Exit slip	
◆ Ask students to recall previous information and relate it to this lesson	◆ Ask students to summarize the lesson	

8. I am aware of the networks, systems, and organization of knowledge.
9. I practice professionalism.
10. I understand the cumulative nature of knowledge.

So, do you have what it takes to meet this challenge?

Questions to Consider

1. Is your classroom student centered or teacher directed?
2. How does differentiated instruction differ from traditional classroom instruction?
3. How might traditional teaching practices result in lower achievement or disengagement of some students from school?
4. How does the teacher use diagnostic and formative assessments to guide instructional decisions?
5. How has your thinking about diversity changed as a result of this book?

Strategies for Teachers

♦ Administer a student interest inventory.
♦ Ask students to list their top three strengths and their top three challenges.
♦ Structure your lesson in 10–15 minute segments. Lessons should be brisk, focused, and engaging.
♦ Use a variety of pedagogical strategies and materials to meet the needs of diverse learners.
♦ Pose different types of questions to prompt higher order thinking. You can find a quick reference to Bloom's Taxonomy levels along with key words, questions, and suggested assessments at https://www.bloomstaxonomy.org/Blooms%20Taxonomy%20questions.pdf.
♦ Provide a menu of options for student assignments, which are all focused on the same objective, but appeal to different interests and strengths.

◆ Invite students to participate in literature circles. Provide four to six sets of novels on different reading levels, but all based on the same subject, i.e., escape, adventure, survival, etc. You can assign students to groups based on reading levels or allow them to self-select their books.

◆ Offer a digital storytelling assignment (Edwards, 2016) which requires students conceptualize content and present key ideas using pictures, text, video, audio, and music. Students may wish to use Voki.com to create a talking animated avatar; Animoto.com to convert still pictures to video; and Storybird.com to create a digital storybook.

◆ Offer a digital poster assignment (Edwards, 2016). Students could create a multimedia interactive poster using edu.glogster.com.

◆ Think outside the Powerpoint—students can use Prezi. com or Voicethread.com to create digital presentations. Or, they could use Fakebook (available on classtools.net) to present biographical material.

◆ Provide multiple assessment options with the same goal or outcome, so students can choose how they want to be assessed.

◆ Facilitate a discussion on how Universal Design for Learning (UDL) affects your classroom and learning.

References

Benjamin, A. (2002). *Differentiated instruction: A guide for middle and high school teachers*. New York, NY: Routledge.

Blaz, D. (2013). *Differentiated assessment for middle and high school classrooms*. New York, NY: Routledge.

Edwards, S. (2016). *Active learning in the middle grades classroom*. Westerville, OH: Association for Middle Level Education.

Tomlinson, C. A. (2014). *The differentiated classroom: Responding to the needs of all learners* (2nd ed.). Alexandria, VA: ASCD.

Wormelli, R. (2007). *Differentiation: From planning to practice, grades 6–12*. Portland, ME: Stenhouse Publishers.

Conclusion

In this book, we have examined different dimensions of diversity, but our students do not fit neatly into one social category or group. A black female, for example, may face challenges because she is black, and also because she is female. Moreover, the intersectionality of multiple social identities is cumulative and complex. The concept of intersectionality focuses attention on the overlapping and conflicting dynamics of race, gender, class, and other social identities in the context of power and structures of inequality (Cho, Crenshaw, & McCall, 2013). In short, we must avoid generalizing, oversimplifying, or making assumptions about the lived experiences of our students. Every student is unique.

With all these concerns in mind, we strive to provide a safe haven in schools with a climate which allows personal growth, academic achievement, and intellectual development, where middle-level students know they can develop close, caring, and trusting relationships with teachers, parents, peers, and their communities. Middle-level students are changing at such a rapid rate, not only from year to year, but from day to day, in all areas—physical, intellectual, emotional, and social. They are experimenting with all types of venues, sexuality, drugs, and relationships. If adults do not provide the cushion young adults need, they will surely be at risk of slipping through the cracks. In *A Tribe Apart*, Patricia Hersch (2013) completed an extensive study of eight teenagers in Reston, Virginia, over a period of three years. Her conclusions are that teens are indeed "a tribe apart." She states, "adults have pulled away, relinquishing responsibility and supervision, allowing the unhealthy behaviors of teens to flourish" (front flap). By becoming totally familiar with the teens in her study, she was able to observe in the most fundamental ways their routines and functions, as well as listen to their thoughts and ideas, their fears, and their questions. While most of us cannot spend either the time or the energy to replicate Hersch's study, we can learn as much as possible about the young people we deal with each day.

What about the boisterous middle schooler down the street? Do we brand him as trouble just because he is an adolescent who has so much excess energy that he runs everywhere he goes? So what if he has long hair and an earring—does this mean he is "trouble?" Do we take the time to get to know him? A middle school student once told her teacher she wore too much makeup and dyed her hair purple just to see how others would react. Makeup and hair dye can be washed off, but if young people get a permanent label just because they experimented with clothes and style, they will indeed become more likely to "fall through the cracks." Middle schoolers can be fascinating, funny, and fantastic young people if given a chance—a chance to know people care about them and what they are doing, a chance to safely experiment with ideas and inspirations, and a chance to search for the meanings of who they are and who we think they are. Van Hoose, Strahan, and L'Esperance (2009) came to this conclusion:

> Young adolescents form a healthy sense of identity when they can address their needs for competence, autonomy, and social support. In spite of their apparent buoyancy, they are fragile, perhaps more fragile than at any other time in their lives. ...the most successful schools and the most successful teachers in the middle grades are those who meet young adolescents' needs for security, support, and success in a proactive manner. (p. 63)

Schools are more diverse—and in ways we would never have imagined possible—than ever before. Because we are now and will continue to become more and more mobile, picking up and moving with job transfers, or seeking new adventures with educational opportunities and retirement, we no longer stay in our hometowns generation after generation with people like us. Today, young people must adjust to a different way of life.

Because of the large percentage of families with two working parents, or families with only one parent who is also a working parent, no longer is there always someone at home after school to greet youngsters with, "How did your day go?" Many times, there is no one to help with homework, no one to answer questions, no one to simply be there at the end of the day.

When young adolescents have questions about the new kid who just moved to town and is in their class, we need to stop and think just who this new kid is. Is he the new kid who is of a different race, a different culture, and who eats unusual foods and dresses differently? Or the new kid whose family lives in its car because dad lost his job and they can't afford to pay rent? Or the new kid who is part of the school inclusion team and has been assigned the seat across the aisle? How we address those questions helps shape our students' perceptions. Our answers must be in the best interest of the new kid and the young adolescent with the questions. Deciding that "different" is wrong because no one has a better definition will only diminish the potential learning experience of both the adolescent and the new student.

It has been said children have to learn to hate, and hate is not a natural condition. If that is the case, it is critical to work with the families and communities of young adolescents, providing examples where people of all differences learn to get along with each other and accept each other as human beings. Many times, parents are reluctant to come to school conferences simply because they do not understand English. Their "difference" sets them apart from the rest of the community, and they do not feel comfortable attending family nights or other parent conference meetings. One school district with a large number of Latino families sends notices of school activities home in both English and Spanish, assuring the message is understood. On the night of the activity, an interpreter is available to ensure everyone understands and participates. This positive action creates a win-win situation for all involved!

Over the past few years, more programs have been developed to help teachers and students find ways to answer some of these questions, establish a sense of family when there are

so many different members, and help young adolescents learn to work with one another in a safe and caring space because of and in spite of their differences. Many schools use email, web services such as Google Classroom, or apps such as The Homework App or Remind to post homework assignments. This is especially helpful if a student has been home ill or absent from school for any other reason.

How Can We Improve the Way We Address Diversity in Middle Schools?

There are a number of ways we can address diversity in middle schools to make them better places to learn. Teachers must recognize their own prejudices and biases. We simply must eliminate phrases, thoughts, and perceptions such as these: "He comes from the other side of town, down by the trailer park. Those kids don't do very well in school." "Remember his brother? No one in that family is very bright." "You know how those Latino kids are. Here today, gone tomorrow. No use in spending extra time with them." What chance do students with such labels have to become successful? We must address these biases when we hear them. We must be willing to speak up when we hear anyone degrading another. And we must take advantage of such occurrences to teach ourselves that as members of the human race, each of us deserves consideration and respect.

One middle school in Colorado with Latino and African American students recognized that reducing conflict was vital so students could focus their energies on acquiring knowledge and prepare for a high school education. A team of teachers organized a culture study which extended across the curriculum to emphasize what each culture has contributed to humanity. They further worked on reducing conflict by recognizing the multiethnic components in everyone's background. It is not enough to say that all students are different. It is not enough to try and understand what makes them different. Teachers must somehow reach students from all kinds of backgrounds and knit together a cohesive community of learners in an atmosphere of caring and mutual respect. Emphasizing, as the Colorado team did, what each culture had contributed to humanity is one way to do this.

The Dove Counterbalance Test was developed in 1968 to illustrate that standardized intelligence tests are biased. Test questions were based on phrasing, actions, and experiences relevant to African American inner-city culture. African Americans would most likely score well on this test, while young people from other backgrounds might not score as well (Groth-Marnet, 2003). Likewise, it should be understood young adolescents who grow up in an African American culture may not do as well on standardized tests used in schools today. There are many ways to say the same thing. If we are to address diversity in our classrooms, we must find different methods of evaluation to reach all of our students.

Connecting with Service Learning

Finally, service learning is a wonderful way to connect our students not only to the community, but in many cases, to those who may be less fortunate. Children in Head Start programs, children having trouble reading, adults who want to learn to read and write but are embarrassed to ask for help, the elderly couple who need their gutters cleaned—these are only a few of the projects middle-level students can become involved in to help those in need. A seventh-grade class in Maine helped to remove old tires from a former dump site. Not only did the students rid the area of unsightly old tires, they also eliminated a potential breeding ground for mosquitoes, an important contribution to the community.

Service learning is an excellent vehicle by which young adolescents can learn more about themselves, discover how they can become useful citizens in their communities, and learn about other members of the community who may be disadvantaged and need help. Service learning provides a connection to real life, which teaches young adolescents they can learn in different places and in different ways than just in the classroom. The benefits of service learning for young adolescents as they progress through their school years and into adulthood include:

◆ Awareness of community problems and needs
◆ Planning, collaboration, and cooperation

◆ Working as a group toward a common goal
◆ Taking active roles to meet real needs of others
◆ Sense of self-worth and personal responsibility
◆ Having an opportunity to reflect critically on experiences

Throughout this book, we have described young adolescents—physically, intellectually, emotionally, and socially—and explained many of the routes they travel during this challenging time in their lives. It is important to celebrate their lives, all the joys, frustrations, "falling downs and getting ups," their triumphs, and even their losses, as these experiences will help them grow and develop into successful young adults. Diversity is an issue we are all faced with daily, whether in the community, the classroom, or the workplace. Therefore, strategies and activities have been included in this book to assist readers in dealing with this difficult task. There are questions, problems, "whys and why nots," and some answers and solutions. Can we find solutions which will be positive for all concerned? We think we can. If each individual is committed to change as he or she learns, much progress can be made. If we continue to research, to study, and to care about each other, and then actually put our ideas into action, we believe we can find ways where everyone can benefit. We must keep trying! We must keep educating! We must keep caring!

Strategies for Teachers

◆ Pair middle school students with "near-peer" tutors. Contact the local high school or a nearby university to engage tutors.
◆ Pair middle school students with younger students as reading buddies or tutors.
◆ Use an advisory meeting to address and discuss social issues concerning young adolescents.
◆ "Be where you don't have to be." Attend school dances, athletic contests, non-athletic events, social and academic events to let the students know you care about them and are interested in them.

◆ Create an after-school program for middle schoolers. Student teachers in one Virginia county work two afternoons a week with middle-grade students, who need extra academic and social skills help. The first half hour is devoted to academic help with homework, and the second half hour is recreational where the student teachers and the students get to know each other on a more personal level.

◆ Ask your students to write a letter to a rising sixth-grade student with advice on how to handle middle school.

References

Cho, S., Crenshaw, K., & McCall, L. (2013). Toward a field of intersectionality studies: Theory, applications, and praxis. *Signs: Intersectionality: Theorizing Power, Empowering Theory, 38*(4), 785–810.

Groth-Marnat, G. (2003). *Handbook of psychological assessment* (4th ed.). Hoboken, NJ: John Wiley & Sons.

Hersch, P. (2013). *A tribe apart: A journey into the heart of American adolescence.* New York, NY: Random House.

Van Hoose, J., Strahan, D., & L'Esperance, M. (2009). *Promoting harmony: Young adolescent development and school practices* (3rd ed.). Westerville, OH: National Middle School Association.

Recommended Adolescent Literature (Current)

Abdel-Fattah, R. (2017). *The lines we cross*. New York, NY: Scholastic.

Michael doesn't question his family's anti-immigrant politics until he meets Mina, an Afghani refugee who is funny, smart, and beautiful.

Albertalli, B. (2015). *Simon vs. The homo sapiens agenda*. New York, NY: Harper Collins.

Simon is a gay teen who's being blackmailed. He forgot to sign out of his email and a classmate discovered the secret messages he was sending anonymously to a teen boy he only knows as Blue, who's also in the closet. Now, if Simon wants his sexuality to stay a secret, he must help that classmate try to hook up with a girl he likes.

Alexie, S. (2009). *The absolutely true diary of a part-time Indian*. New York, NY: Little, Brown and Company.

Junior is a teenage aspiring cartoonist growing up on a Spokane Indian reservation. He decides to break away to attend an all-white school where the only other Indian is the school mascot.

Altebrando, T. (2016). *The leaving.* New York, NY: Bloomsbury Publishing.

Six kindergarteners were taken. Eleven years later, five come back, with no idea of where they've been. No one remembers the sixth victim, Max Avery. Max's sister needs to find her brother—dead or alive—and isn't buying this whole memory-loss story.

Angleberger, T. (2010). *The strange case of Origami Yoda.* New York, NY: Amulet Books, Scholastic.

Funny, uncannily wise portrait of the dynamics of a sixth-grade class and of the greatness that sometimes comes in unlikely packages. Dwight is the class oddball who talks to his classmates via an origami finger puppet of Yoda. Origami Yoda is smart, makes predictions, and saves a classmate from embarrassment with amazingly correct advice.

Collins, S. (2008). *The hunger games* (series). New York, NY: Scholastic.

In what was once North America, the capital of Panem maintains its hold on its twelve districts by forcing them each to select a boy and a girl, called Tributes, to compete in a nationally televised annual event called the Hunger Games. Every citizen must watch as the youths fight to the death until only one remains. Will sixteen-year-old Katniss Everdeen survive the Games?

Condie, A. (2010). *Matched.* New York, NY: Dutton Books.

Dystopian young adult novel about a tightly-controlled society in which young people are "matched" with their life partners at the age of 17.

Dashner, J. (2014). *The maze runner.* New York, NY: Delacorte Press.

Thomas wakes up in a metal elevator that brings him to a place called *The Glade.* He has no memory of who he is or how he got there. He gradually discovers the Glade is run by two boys, who both maintain order by enforcing simple but effective rules. The elevator box surfaces from under the ground every week supplying new food, tools, medicines, and sometimes weapons. Every month a new boy with no memory of anything but his first name finds himself in the elevator box.

Forman, G. (2014). *If I stay*. New York, NY: Dutton Books for Young Readers.

A talented young cellist thought the most difficult decision she would ever have to make would be whether to pursue her musical dreams at prestigious Julliard or follow her heart to be with the love of her life, a rock singer/guitarist. However, a car wreck changes everything in an instant, and now her life hangs in the balance. Suspended between life and death, she faces a choice that will decide her future.

Gratz, A. (2017). *Refugee*. New York, NY: Scholastic.

Josef is a Jewish boy living in 1930s Nazi Germany. With the threat of concentration camps looming, he and his family board a ship bound for the other side of the world. Isabel is a Cuban girl in 1994. With riots and unrest plaguing her country, she and her family set out on a raft, hoping to find safety in America. Mahmoud is a Syrian boy in 2015. With his homeland torn apart by violence and destruction, he and his family begin a long trek toward Europe. As the three young people and their families go in search of refuge, they face unimaginable dangers from drownings to bombings to betrayals. But, there is always the hope of tomorrow.

Green, J. (2012). *The fault in our stars*. New York, NY: Dutton Books.

Hazel Grace Lancaster has been living with cancer for three of her seventeen years of life. Despite this, she is a girl with a vibrant mind, biting wit, and incredible empathy for her parents who have to care for her.

Green, J. (2017). *Turtles all the way down*. New York, NY: Dutton Books.

A powerful narrative about a teen coping with OCD and extreme anxiety.

Grisham, J. (2010). *Theodore Boone: Kid lawyer*. New York, NY: Puffin Books.

Though he's only thirteen years old, Theodore Boone has spent more time in the courtroom than almost anywhere else, and there's always a new adventure waiting.

Hamilton, B., & Bundschuh, R. (2011). *Soul surfer*. New York, NY: Simon & Schuster.

A 13-year-old girl lost her arm to a shark. She describes the frightening attack, but also talks about how she persevered after her injury. Only a month later, she learned to surf again and then returned to pro surfing.

Kinney, J. (2007). *Diary of a wimpy kid*. (series). New York, NY: Scholastic.

A satirical realistic fiction comedy about a boy named Greg Heffley and his attempts to become popular in middle school.

Levine, K. (2002). *Hana's suitcase*. New York, NY: Scholastic.

A Japanese woman is determined to uncover the identity and destiny of the owner of a suitcase sent by a Holocaust museum. Her investigation takes her around the world before she finally solves the mystery, while using the journey to teach her students about the tragedy of the Holocaust.

Palacio, R. J. (2017). *Wonder*. New York, NY: Alfred A. Knopf.

Ten-year-old Auggie, born with extreme facial abnormalities, goes from being home-schooled to entering a private middle school, where he endures taunts and teasing. He has to deal with so much he wonders if he will ever make friends.

Patterson, J., & Tebbetts, C. (2011). *Middle school, the worst years of my life*. New York, NY: Little, Brown and Company.

This story follows sixth-grader, Rafe Khatchadorian, as he begins middle school and copes with the awkwardness of adolescence, including rushes, bullying, and family issues. He attempts to break every school rule and collect the most points any student has ever been given.

Riordan, R. (2005). *The lightning thief*. New York, NY: Miramax Books, Puffin Books.

Twelve-year-old Percy Jackson is on the most dangerous quest of his life. He must journey across the United States to catch a thief, who has stolen the original weapon of mass destruction—Zeus' master bolt.

Roth, V. (2014). *Divergent*. New York, NY: Harper Collins.

In a world divided by factions based on virtues, Tris learns she's Divergent and won't fit in. When she discovers a plot to destroy Divergents, Tris and the mysterious Four must find out what makes Divergents dangerous before it's too late.

Swanson, J. L. (2009). *Chasing Lincoln's killer*. New York: Scholastic Press.

The 12-day chase for Lincoln's killer shows young people's version of an accessible look at the assassination of a president and shows readers Abraham Lincoln—the man, the father, the husband, and the friend—and how his death impacted those closest to him.

Thomas, A. (2018). *The hate U give*. New York, NY: Harper Collins.

Sixteen-year-old Starr Carter moves between two worlds—the poor neighborhood where she lives, and the fancy suburban prep school she attends. The uneasy balance between these worlds is shattered when she witnesses the fatal shooting of her childhood best friend, Khalil, at the hands of a police officer.

Watson, R. (2010). *What Momma left me.* New York, NY: Bloomsbury.

Thirteen-year-old Serenity and her younger brother must go live with their grandparents when their mother is killed. The teen struggles, but gains strength from the family and the community.

Watson, R. (2017). *Piecing me together.* New York, NY: Bloomsbury.

Jade is a gifted black girl who attends a mostly white school on scholarship. She appreciates her many opportunities, but is tired of people stereotyping and trying to "fix" her.

Woodson, J. (2014). *Brown girl dreaming.* New York, NY: Puffin Books.

Through this collection of poems, the author shares what it was like to grow up as an African American girl in the 1960s and 1970s, living with the remnants of Jim Crow and her growing awareness of the Civil Rights movement.

Yoon, N. (2016). *The sun is also a star.* New York, NY: Delacorte Press.

A teenage undocumented immigrant from Jamaica meets a Korean American boy 24 hours before she's about to be deported with the rest of her family.

Zusak, M. (2007). *The book thief.* New York, NY: Alfred A. Knopf.

This story is narrated by a compassionate Death, who tells us about Liesel, a foster girl living outside of Munich, who scratches out a meager existence for herself by stealing when she encounters something she can't resist—books. With the help of her accordion-playing foster father, she learns to read and shares her stolen books with her neighbors during bombing raids as well as with the Jewish man hidden in her basement.

B

Recommended Adolescent Literature (Classics)

Anonymous (1998). *Go ask Alice.* New York, NY: Aladdin.

A true story of a 15-year-old girl's descent into the world of drugs presented in the form of her diary.

Armstrong, W. H. (1971). *Sour land.* New York. NY: Scholastic.

Anson Stone is a white widower with three children. A black male teacher enters their lives and fills a lonely void, but helps them face a tragic reality.

Arrick, F. (1992). *What you don't know can kill you.* New York, NY: Bantam Doubleday.

Debra's "perfect" older sister discovers she is HIV positive, and her dreams of college and marriage to her wonderful boyfriend are shattered. This story tells how she and her family handle the tragedy.

Bauer, M. (1986). *Am I blue? Coming out from the silence.* New York, NY: Harper Trophy.

Short stories about growing up gay or lesbian from authors, Bruce Coville, M. E. Kerr, William Sleator, Jane Valen, and others.

Beatty, P. (1981). *Lupita manana.* New York, NY: Beech Tree Books.

Thirteen-year-old Lupita decides to cross the border into the United States as an illegal alien to help her poverty-stricken family.

Beatty, P. (1992). *Who comes with cannons?* New York, NY: Morrow.

The start of the Civil War changes the world of Truth, a 12-year-old Quaker girl from Indiana who is staying with relatives in North Carolina.

Benjamin, C. I. (1984). *Nobody's baby now.* New York, NY: Bantam Books.

Olivia suddenly not only has to share her room with her ailing grandmother, but she must also babysit her after school instead of spending time with her boyfriend.

Block, F. L. (1995). *Baby Be-Bop.* New York, NY: Harper Collins.

Sixteen-year-old Dirk MacDonald gets ghostly visits from his dead father and great-grandmother, which helps him adjust to being gay.

Brooks, B. (1984). *The moves make the man.* New York, NY: Harper Row.

A precarious friendship forms between an African American boy and an emotionally disturbed white boy.

Bunting, E. (1989). *The Wednesday surprise.* Boston, MA: Houghton Mifflin.

Anna stays with her grandmother every Wednesday night. As a surprise to her family, Anna is teaching her grandmother to read.

Buss, F. L., & Cubias, D. (1991). *Journey of the sparrows.* New York, NY: Dutton.

Illegal Salvadoran refugees struggle trying to make a living in Chicago after they have been smuggled into the U.S. in crates.

Collier, J. L., & Collier, C. (1994). *With every drop of blood*. New York, NY: Bantam Doubleday.

A friendship develops during the Civil War between an African American Union soldier and the 14-year-old white boy who is transporting food to Richmond, Virginia.

Conley, J. L. (1993). *Crazy lady*. New York, NY: Harper Collins.

A story of the developing relationship between an alcoholic mother and her retarded son with a young man who had previously teased them and treated them disrespectfully.

Crutcher, C. (1993). *Staying fat for Sarah Byrnes*. New York, NY: Bantam Doubleday.

Two young people—one boy and one girl—are the "terminal uglies" and inseparable best friends. This book tells of the trials and tribulations of their friendship and how they survived.

Duffy, J. (1993). *Radical red*. New York, NY: Charles Scribner.

Family abuse drives an Irish mother and daughter to work with Susan B. Anthony and the suffragette movement.

Ellis, S. (1994). *Out of the blue*. New York, NY: Penguin Puffin Books.

After she discovers she has a 24-year-old half-sister, 12-year old Megan tracks down her mother to see why she was never told about her sister.

Gallo, D. R. (1993). *Join in multiethnic short stories by outstanding writers for young adults*. New York, NY: Delacorte Press.

Several stories that reflect views of young adults of various ethnic backgrounds on friendship and prejudice.

Gibson, W. (1960). *The miracle worker.* New York, NY: Bantam Books.

The story of Helen Keller and her teacher, Annie Sullivan.

Greene, B. (1973). *Summer of my German soldier.* New York, NY: Bantam Doubleday Books.

Twelve-year-old Patty Bergen is Jewish. She befriends a young German prison escapee when her small hometown in Arkansas becomes the site of a German prisoner of war camp in World War II.

Greene, B. (1991). *The drowning of Stephan Jones.* New York, NY: Bantam Books.

A young girl, Carla, struggles with her boyfriend's harassment of the homosexual owners of an antique shop. She and the other young people in town deal with the tragic ending of this harassment.

Greene, S. (1979). *The boy who drank too much.* New York, NY: Laurel Leaf Books.

A young teenage boy is not dealing well with his alcoholic father and the fact his mother has died. He too begins the long, lonely road of destroying himself with alcohol.

Guy, R. (1973). *The friends.* New York, NY: Bantam Books.

Phyllisia, a 14-year-old from the West Indies, is overwhelmed by her new life in New York. Needing a friend, she meets up with white, 15-year-old Edith, a New York ragamuffin.

Hansen, J. (1980). *The gift giver.* New York, NY: Clarion.

Doris, a fifth-grader, meets a special friend in her Bronx neighborhood, and they decide not to always go along with the crowd.

Heron, A., & Maran, M. (1991). *How would you feel if your dad was gay?* Boston, MA: Alyson Publications.

This book relates the struggles of children who let their friends know a parent is gay.

Hesse, K. (1997). *Out of the dust.* New York, NY: Scholastic.

In a series of poems, 15-year-old Billie Jo relates her life in the Dustbowl years of the Depression in Oklahoma.

Hinton, S. E. (1967). *The outsiders.* New York, NY: Viking Press.

A teen gang in Oklahoma, the Greasers, are perpetually at odds with the Socials, a rival group. When two Greasers get into a brawl that ends in the death of a Social member, the boys are forced to go into hiding. Soon the Greasers must contend with the consequences of their violent lives.

Hobbs., W. (1988). *Changes in latitude.* New York, NY: Avon Flare Books.

A family vacation in Mexico leads to a nightmare of discovery of the parents' problems, tragedy in saving endangered species of turtles, and anger and betrayal. The book also deals with the young man's change from a cocky selfish young man to one who wants to understand and be of help.

Hobbs, W. (1991). *Downriver.* New York, NY: Bantam Books.

Rebellious teenagers, formerly enrolled in a wilderness survival school team, "borrow" rafting equipment from their adult leader, steal his boots, and head for the Colorado River and the Grand Canyon rapids.

Hunt, I. (1976). *The lottery rose.* New York, NY: Berkley Publishing.

Georgie Burgess is abused by his alcoholic mother and her boyfriends. He wins a small rosebush in a grocery store lottery, giving him the impetus to survive.

Irwin, H. (1987). *Kim/Kimi*. New York, NY: Puffin Books.

Sixteen-year-old Kim/Kimi, a Japanese-American, struggles to find her identity in an all-white Iowa community.

Kassam, L. (1986). *Middle school blues*. New York, NY: Avon Camelot Books.

After deciding middle school was like landing in the middle of a bad dream, Cindy decides to write a guidebook on how to get through it.

Kassam, L. (1993). *Odd one out*. New York, NY: Fawcett Juniper Books.

Alison Gray is bright, pretty, and popular. She is asked to join the exclusive high school sorority club. When her boyfriend tries to win a bet by taking advantage of her, she decides to speak up about what really takes place at the initiations. She learns there is a price to pay.

Krisher, T. (1994). *Spite fences*. New York, NY: Bantam Doubleday.

Changes begin happening to 13-year-old Maggie Pughin during the summer of 1960 in Georgia. Maggie experiences troubles with her mother and is drawn into the violence, hatred, and racial tension.

Krumgold, J. (1959). *Onion John*. New York, NY: Scholastic.

Andy Rusch was happy to work in the family hardware store and play on the local baseball team, but his father wanted him to become an engineer.

L'Engle, M. (1962). *A wrinkle in time*. Crosswicks, Ltd., New York, NY: Square Fish.

Meg Murry and her little brother, Charles Wallace, have been without their scientist father for five years, ever since he discovered a new planet and used the concept known as tesseract to travel there. Joined by Meg's classmate and guided by three mysterious astral travers known as Mrs. Whatsit, Mrs. Who, and Mrs. Which, the children brave a dangerous journey to a planet that possesses all of the evil in the universe.

Levine, E., & Nelson, K. (2007). *Henry's freedom box: A true story from the underground railroad*. New York, NY: Scholastic Press.

Henry was a slave and when he climbed into his Freedom Box on the train, he hoped he would be carried to a safe world. He traveled 350 miles from Richmond, VA, to Philadelphia in 27 hours.

Levy, M. (1990). *Rumors and whispers*. New York, NY: Ballantine/Fawcett.

Sarah Alexander, a high school senior, must learn to deal with moving from Ohio to California, with the sudden disowning of her brother for reasons she cannot find out, and her favorite art teacher being fired because he has AIDS.

Lorbiecki, M. (1998). *Sister Anne's hands*. New York, NY: Dial Books for Young Readers.

Poetic, understated prose and luminous paintings loaded with period detail, enhance this story about how a teacher can change a child's life.

Lowry, L. (1993). *The giver*. New York, NY: Dell.

At the Ceremony of Twelve, Jonas receives the memories shared by only one other member of his community. He discovers the society he lives in is not as perfect as he once thought.

Mazer, N. (1984). *Mrs. Fish, Ape, and me, the Dump Queen*. New York, NY: Avon.

A young girl's uncle runs the town dump, which causes her to be teased every day. She finally becomes friends with Mrs. Fish, the school custodian, who helps her survive.

Meyer, C. (1993). *White lilacs*. New York, NY: Harcourt Brace.

In 1921 in Dillion, Texas, 12-year-old Rose Lee, her family, and her neighborhood are forced to relocate when the whites in town decide to build a park where they live.

Miklowtz, G. (1986). *The war between the classes*. New York, NY: Dell.

Emiko, 17-old Japanese American, has fallen in love with white, blond Adam. Traditions and cultures are major issues in their relationship.

Mohr, N. (1989). *El Bronx remembered*. Houston, TX: Arte Publico Press.

Puerto Rican families living in the Bronx tell of their experiences of owning a pet hen named after their favorite Hollywood movie star, gypsies telling the future, and a young boy's humiliation at his graduation.

Newman, L. (1994). *Fat chance*. New York, NY: Paper Star Book.

Judi Liebowitz wants to be the "thinnest girl in the entire eighth-grade," until she becomes "friends" with Nancy Pratt who suffers secretly from binge-and-purge cycles of bulimia.

Paterson, K. (1991). *Lyddie*. New York, NY: Penguin.

In the 1840s, Lyddie's parents have died, and her siblings have been sent to live with other people. Lyddie is determined to work in the factory in Lowell, Massachusetts, to make enough money to reunite her family.

Paulsen, G. (1987). *Hatchet*. New York, NY: Delacorte Press.

Thirteen-year-old Brian, whose parents are divorced, survives a plane crash in the Canadian wilderness en route to visit his father. He must use the hatchet his mother once gave him to stay alive.

Paulsen, G. (1993). *Nightjohn*. New York, NY: Delacorte Press.

Twelve-year-old Sarney's life as a female slave becomes even more dangerous when a newly arrived slave offers to teach her to read.

Philip, M. (1988). *Harriet's daughter*. Toronto: The Women's Press.

Immigration, exile, culture, and identity all combine in this story of Margaret trying to help her friend escape from Canada and live with her grandmother in Tobago.

Rosen, M. (1995). *A school for Pompey Walker*. New York, NY: Harcourt Brace Jovanovich.

An old former slave, Pompey, relates how his white friend kept selling him into slavery to earn money to build a school.

Scott, V. (1986). *Belonging*. Washington, DC: Galludet College Press.

The adjustments and reactions by a 15-year-old girl who has become deaf after recovering from meningitis.

Sebestyen, O. (1968). *Words by heart*. New York, NY: Bantam Doubleday.

Lena wants her classmates to know her for her "magic mind" rather than her black skin. After experiencing violence and death, she must learn how to forgive.

Shannon, G. (1989). *Unlived affections*. New York, NY: Harper and Row.

At his grandmother's death, 18-year-old Willie discovers many family secrets, including the fact his father is gay.

Silverstein, S. (2014, 1974). *Where the sidewalk ends*. New York, NY: Harper Collins.

A humorous collection of poems and drawings by Shel Silverstein. You'll find a boy who turns into a TV set, a girl who eats a whale, and Sarah Cynthia Sylvia Stout who will not take the garbage out. It is a place where you wash your shadow and plant diamond gardens, a place where shoes fly, little sisters are auctioned off, and crocodiles go to the dentist.

Soto, G. (1991). *Taking sides.* San Diego, CA: Harcourt Brace Jovanovich.

Lincoln Mendoza has moved from the barrio to the tree-lined streets of the suburbs and finds himself playing basketball against his old friends.

Soto, G. (1993). *Pool party.* New York, NY: Delacorte Press.

Rudy Herrera is surprised and excited to get an invitation to a pool party from Tiffany Perez, the richest and most popular girl in school.

Speare, E. (1958). *The witch of Blackbird Pond.* Boston, MA: Houghton Mifflin.

Kit, a young girl from the Caribbean, is orphaned and sent to New England to live with relatives. In a time of the Salem Witch Trials, she is seen as suspicious.

Tolkien, J. R. R. (2005, 1955). *The lord of the rings* (series). New York, NY: Houghton Mifflin Harcourt.

Saga of a group of sometimes reluctant heroes who set forth to save their world from consummate evil. The Lord of the Rings tells of the great quest undertaken by Frodo and the Fellowship of the Ring: Gandalf the Wizard; the hobbits Merry, Pippin, and Sam; Gimli the Dwarf; Legolas the Elf; Boromir of Gondor; and a tall, mysterious stranger called Strider.

Its many worlds and creatures were drawn from Tolkien's extensive knowledge of philology and folklore.

Voight, C. (1981). *Dicey's song.* New York, NY: Scholastic.

Dicey's story of taking care of her three younger siblings while traveling from Provincetown to Chesapeake Bay to their grandmother's house. Dicey discovers she needs a lot of love, trust, humor, and courage.

Voight, C. (1982). *Homecoming.* New York, NY: Scholastic.

After being deserted by both her mother and father, 13-year-old Dicey searches for someone who will take her in and care for her and her three siblings.

Voight, C. (1983). *A solitary blue.* New York, NY: Scholastic.

Jeff's mother left him with his father. She disappeared for several years. When she suddenly invited him to come visit her, Jeff started to open up and feel again. Was that a mistake?

Voight, C. (1994). *When she hollers.* New York, NY: Scholastic.

Tish's adoptive stepfather has been abusing her since she was a small child. Now she is determined to do something to stop it.

Walter, M. (1982). *Girl on the outside.* New York, NY: Scholastic.

Two girls—one white and one African American—are caught up in the flurry of the 1957 integration of all-white Chatman High School in the small southern town of Mossville.

Wartski, M. (1980). *A boat to nowhere.* New York, NY: Signet Books.

Mai, her little brother, and grandfather join a 14-year-old boy on a journey aboard a small boat from their village in Vietnam to safety.

Williams-Garcia, R. (1992). *Fast talk on a slow track.* New York, NY: Dutton/ Lodestar.

Denzel Watson, a black honors student, spends the summer before college trying to raise money by selling candy. He learns a lesson in motivation and how to apply himself.

Willis, P. (1995). *Out of the storm*. New York, NY: Avon Books.

Mandy and her mother are forced to move in with "cranky Aunt Bess" after Mandy's father died in World War II. A crisis turns Mandy's life around and helps her dream new dreams.

Woodson, J. (1993). *The dear one*. New York, NY: Dell.

Twelve-year-old Ferri is having to learn to adjust to a 15-year-old pregnant teenager who has come to live with her family.

Yeo, W. (1986). *Gypsy summer*. New York, NY: Scholastic Books.

Katy and her brother Walter meet Marya, a Gypsy girl who is in town for the summer. After a rough start, the three become friends and Katy looks forward to Marya returning the next summer.

Association for Middle Level Education Standards

Issues pertaining to diversity are prominently featured in the Middle Level Teacher Preparation Standards (2012) of the Association for Middle Level Education (AMLE). AMLE's standards and elements related to diversity are as follows:

Standard 1

Element b. Knowledge of the Implications of Diversity on Young Adolescent Development: Middle-level teacher candidates demonstrate their understanding of the implications of diversity on the development of young adolescents. They implement curriculum and instruction that is responsive to young adolescents' local, national, and international histories, language/dialects, and individual identities (e.g., race, ethnicity, culture, age, appearance, ability, sexual orientation, socioeconomic status, family composition). They participate successfully in middle-level practices that consider and celebrate the diversity of all young adolescents.

Standard 3

Element b. Middle Level Organization and Best Practices: Middle-level teacher candidates utilize their knowledge of the effective components of middle-level programs and schools to foster equitable educational practices and to enhance learning for all students (e.g., race, ethnicity, culture, age, appearance, ability, sexual orientation, socioeconomic status, family composition).

Standard 5

Element c. Working with Family Members and Community Involvement: Middle-level teacher candidates understand and value the ways diverse family structures and cultural backgrounds influence and enrich learning. They communicate and collaborate with all family members and community partners, and participate in school and community activities. They engage in practices that build positive, collaborative relationships with families from diverse cultures and backgrounds (e.g., race, ethnicity, culture, age, appearance, ability, sexual orientation, socioeconomic status, family composition).

D

AMLE Essential Attributes and Characteristics

In its 2021 position paper, *The Successful Middle School: This We Believe*, the Association for Middle Level Education (AMLE) describes essential attributes and characteristics of successful schools. AMLE affirms that an education for young adolescents must be:

1. **Responsive:** Using the distinctive nature and identities of young adolescents as the foundation upon which all decisions about school are made.
2. **Challenging:** Cultivating high expectations and advancing learning for every member of the school community.
3. **Empowering:** Facilitating environments in which students take responsibility for their own learning and contribute positively to the world around them.
4. **Equitable:** Providing socially just learning opportunities and environments for every student.
5. **Engaging:** Fostering a learning atmosphere that is relevant, participatory, and motivating for all learners.

Characteristics of Successful Schools

AMLE believes that these five essential attributes of successful middle-level education can be realized and achieved best through 18 characteristics which are grouped in three categories—Culture and Community; Curriculum, Instruction, and Assessment; and Leadership and Organization. The characteristics are interdependent and need to be implemented in concert.

Culture and Community

- Educators respect and value young adolescents.
- The school environment is welcoming, inclusive, and affirming for all.
- Every student's academic and personal development is guided by an adult advocate.
- School safety is addressed proactively, justly, and thoughtfully.
- Comprehensive counseling and support services meet the needs of young adolescents.
- The school engages families as valued partners.
- The school collaborates with community and business partners.

Curriculum, Instruction, and Assessment

- Educators are specifically prepared to teach young adolescents and possess a depth of understanding in the content areas they teach.
- Curriculum is challenging, exploratory, integrative, and diverse.
- Health, wellness, and social-emotional competence are supported in curricula, school-wide programs, and related policies.
- Instruction fosters learning that is active, purposeful, and democratic.
- Varied and ongoing assessments advance learning as well as measure it.

Leadership and Organization

- A shared vision developed by all stakeholders guides every decision.

- ◆ Policies and practices are student-centered, unbiased, and fairly implemented.
- ◆ Leaders are committed to and knowledgeable about young adolescents, equitable practices, and educational research.
- ◆ Leaders demonstrate courage and collaboration.
- ◆ Professional learning for all staff is relevant, long term, and job-embedded.
- ◆ Organizational structures foster purposeful learning and meaningful relationships.

Source: Bishop, P. A., & Harrison, L. M. (2021). *The successful middle school: This we believe.* Columbus, OH: Association for Middle Level Education.